Why God Hides

Fr. John C. Portavella

Why God Hides
And Where to Find Him

SOPHIA INSTITUTE PRESS
Manchester, New Hampshire

Sophia Institute Press
Box 5284, Manchester, NH 03108
1-800-888-9344

www.SophiaInstitute.com

Sophia Institute Press® is a registered trademark of Sophia Institute.

Library of Congress Cataloging-in-Publication Data

Names: Portavella, John C., author.
Title: Why God hides : and where to find Him / Fr. John C. Portavella.
Other titles: Discovering the hidden God
Description: Manchester, New Hampshire : Sophia Institute Press, 2018.
  Originally published under title: Discovering the hidden God. Pasig City :
  University of Asia and the Pacific, 2014. Includes bibliographical
  references.
Identifiers: LCCN 2018008807 ISBN 9781622825226 (pbk. : alk. paper)
Subjects: LCSH: Hidden God.
Classification: LCC BT180.H54 P67 2018 DDC 231.7—dc23 LC record available at https://lccn.loc.gov/2018008807

First printing

This book is dedicated to
St. Josemaría Escrivá,
Blessed Alvaro del Portillo,
and Bishop Javier Echevarría,
as a token of gratitude for their loving
paternity in successive periods of time.

It is also dedicated to my parents,
José María Portavella
and María Casanova,
who, with awesome faith and
stoutheartedness,
gladly made it possible.

Contents

Foreword

I first met the author of this book, Fr. John C. Portavella, in 1972, when I was taking care of a very small parish in Lipa, Batangas. We subsequently followed separated paths, as he moved to the Visayan region in the south of the Philippines, to carry out his apostolic tasks in Opus Dei. Throughout the years, however, we have maintained bonds of affection, prayer, priestly brotherhood, and fond memories.

Thus, I am now very happy to offer this foreword to his latest work on a topic of universal interest: *the hidden God*.

"Truly you are a God who hides Himself," we read in Isaiah 45:15. It might appear as a puzzling reality that the Almighty would be a silent and hidden witness of the most diverse happenings in the world and in our lives of great accomplishments and of terrible events. On occasion, we might be tempted to wonder why God does not intervene more openly in order to advance a good cause, or to put an end to an evil one. It is what Benedict XVI referred to when he wrote, "One can still ask why God did not make a world in which His presence is more evident — why Christ did not leave the world with another sign of His presence so radiant that no one could resist it. This is the mystery of God and man which we find so inscrutable."[1]

Without pretending to explain or fully decipher what will always remain a mysterious matter, the author presents in this book a number of valuable insights into this intriguing question. After describing our current earthly situation and our very deep longing to see God, which are so vividly expressed in many of the psalms, he describes our life as being, fundamentally, a test of faith. This latter assumption throws abundant light on why the Lord does not normally manifest Himself to us in an open and pellucid manner; and, in summarizing this discourse, the author emphatically states that *this life is for faith, while the next life is for vision.*

In a striking and quite original fashion, Fr. Portavella also views our life as a game played by the hidden God with each of us, and he mentions some of the unwritten rules governing this game.

After considering the way God frequently deals with us, the author points out the pivotal roles played by faith and human freedom in our earthly sojourn. Finally, I am happy that this work comes to light during the Year of Faith, for it could definitely strengthen and revive the faith of many people.

+ Gaudencio B. Cardinal Rosales
Archbishop Emeritus of Manila
2014

---

[1] Benedict XVI, *Jesus of Nazareth* (New York: Doubleday, 2007), 34.

Acknowledgments

I wish to express my heartfelt gratitude to all those who, in different ways, have contributed to the making of this book. I will not attempt, here, to give due credit, nominally, to every one of them. I am sure, though, that God knows their efforts and will not fail to reward them very well. Nonetheless, I think I have to make an exception with Jose Maria Mariano, Ph.D., president of the University of Asia and the Pacific, under whose auspices this book comes to light; with Veronica Esposo Ramirez, Ph.D., CRC director of operations; with Mrs. Erlinda Paez and Divine Angeli P. Endriga, who patiently helped in the editing of this work; with Dr. Paul Dumol, Mr. Marcelo de la Cruz, and Mr. Rafael Lobrin, who gave some of their precious time to the task of reviewing and revising the text; and with the late Col. Eduardo Ungson, Mr. Antonio Jon, Mr. Walter Brown, V. Pacquing Junt, and Mr. Wilson Ledesma, who also contributed to make this project a reality.

May the hidden God repay all of them a hundredfold.

Introduction

Truly, thou art a God who hidest thyself.

—Isaiah 45:15

The experience of wonder is universal. One of the things we wonder about is the hidden Designer, Creator, and Maintainer of the universe. The world is clear and manifest to us, but its Maker, the ultimate Cause of it all, is not. Our reason tells us that He must be there, that He exists, and that He is almighty, omniscient, unchangeable, eternal, and just. It is enough to look at a blooming rose, admire the colors and symmetry of its construction, and sense its fragrance to conclude that it has an intelligent designer and artist. For the beauty of a rose cannot be pure chance. The same is true for the fertilization of flowers by insects with pollen on their legs. Consider too the arrangements in man's optical and hearing systems, the superb activity of the brain, and the splendid immune system of the human body. Could all of them be just chance?

But it is also true that a veil covers God from our sense perceptions. The mind can figure that this is because He is infinite Spirit. The question is: What reason could He have for not manifesting

1

Himself in an open, clear, and perceptible manner, if not always, at least from time to time? There would be a number of advantages to that: the first is that everyone would acknowledge God. Relating to Him would then be easy and a great honor. There would hardly be any sinners daring to disobey His will while He is perceptibly watching.

As things are now, relating to the Almighty is difficult. It is not easy talking with an interlocutor who is almost always silent and invisible. In the course of history, many have ignored Him, yet many others have fervently expressed their desire, with a passion proper to lovers, that the veil covering Him be removed.

God, who is not the object of sense experience, remains silent. When a good deed guided by conscience is done, there is no applause. Conversely, when something is done against conscience, even a terrible crime, there is no external and sensible sign of disapproval.[2]

God appears totally mysterious and beyond the capacity of man to understand. This book attempts to offer some insights into this intriguing mystery, and it ventures answers that might surprise some readers.

In his encyclical *Deus Caritas Est*, Pope Benedict XVI states that God loves with an infinite love. He is a loving Father and the great spectator of life. He is eager to give Himself in an eternal embrace of union, life, vision, and love, which comprises heaven. Since this gift is immense, rational creatures have to pass a test before they can attain the reward. According to Catholic

---

[2] As Cardinal John Henry Newman explained, the inner subjective experience of the "voice of conscience" is a valid demonstration of God's existence. Here, however, I am referring only to the absence of external or sensible signs.

tradition, the angels were subjected to a test at the beginning of creation. The Fathers of the Church concluded that angels, beings like men and rational creatures, underwent some form of trial.

Life is a test for which God endowed man with free will. To ensure the enjoyment of freedom and responsibility, the Almighty refrains from making His presence obvious or too forcefully felt. He wants children, not slaves.

The ultimate reason for God's hiding and His silence is His love. The surprising answer to the query why He hides is that He loves his creatures so much!

The conclusion is this: in his earthly condition, man finds himself separated from God by a veil that only the lights of faith and reason can pierce. The two are gifts that cannot contradict each other. However, the mind has been weakened by sin, so that the natural capacity to understand things needs the supernatural light of faith in order to gain true and valid insights into the mystery of the First Principle of everything.

When the trial is passed, the reward consists in an eternal vision and union with God, a most fitting recompense for those who doggedly walked in darkness and longed to see Him, and said with the psalmist, "Thy face, LORD, do I seek!" (Ps. 27:8).

Everything begins with the love that the eternal Father has for His children, a love so intense that it has prompted Him to grant humans the reward of eternal vision.

1

The Hidden God

He departed and hid himself from them.

—John 12:36

In the beginning, there was brightness in Paradise. The Maker spoke familiarly with Adam and Eve, even if they did not have the Beatific Vision. They were on wonderful terms with the Almighty, but only through His limited apparitions — that is, without showing fully His divinity, as He does in Heaven. Under these circumstances, they could fail Him, and unfortunately, they did.

No sooner had Adam and Eve fallen into sin than they hid themselves from the Maker whose presence they had enjoyed up to that moment, "And they heard the sound of the LORD God walking in the garden in the cool of the day, and the man and the wife hid themselves from the presence of the LORD God among the trees of the garden" (Gen. 3:8). Significantly, it was not the Almighty who hid; our first parents did. Ronald Knox wrote:

> On that miserable day when they sinned and knew that they had sinned, they hid themselves from the presence of the Lord among the trees of the Garden. They did — you

see—what we are always doing: plunged themselves into the midst of creatures in order to forget their Creator. But He called them even so.[3]

This was also true of Cain, who, after slaying Abel, had a dialogue with Yahweh, who asked him: "Where is Abel your brother?" He said, "I do not know; am I my brother's keeper?" And the Lord said, "What have you done? The voice of your brother's blood is crying to me from the ground" (Gen. 4:9–10). The punishment the Lord meted out to Cain was to make him a fugitive and a wanderer on earth (Gen. 4:12), which is, to some extent, the condition of man on earth after the Fall.

From the catastrophic moment of the first sin and man's expulsion from Paradise to the present, the world has been wrapped in darkness. Man's ancestors experienced spiritual blindness, aided only by the diminished light of reason and the sporadic light that came from the successive covenants. These lights were like shining torches in a pitch-black night.

The loss of familiarity with God ranks high among the consequences of original sin, for with the Fall, the familiar God (*Deus familiaris*) became the hidden God (*Deus absconditus*). The tragic change in the Garden of Eden was man's own doing, not Yahweh's. A loving and forgiving Father, He wanted to be near His creatures, but man's misuse of freedom led to his separation from God.

Aside from this important factor that contributed to man's state of unfamiliarity with God, what other possible reasons can God have for remaining concealed?

---

[3] Ronald Knox, *A Retreat for Lay People* (Lagos: Criterion Publishers, 2005), 79.

The Hidden God

Our Vigilance

The Father God is veiled, and He keeps us "in suspense," which is certainly an uncomfortable situation. But it is out of love and mercy that He does so, for this opens many opportunities for man to earn merit.

The offenses against Him, were they committed in His manifest presence, would deserve awesome punishment. It is for this reason that the saints, who had extraordinary experiences of God, were also potentially exceptional sinners.

The present dispensation is a blessing for man, for it keeps him alert. When the apostles asked Jesus about the Second Coming, He answered: "It is not for you to know times or seasons which the Father has fixed by his own authority" (Acts 1:7). The unknown time of the Second Coming kept the disciples of the Lord on their toes and begot in them an attitude of vigilance. Similarly, the "suspense" man experiences in relation to the veiled Father does him much good, for knowing neither the time nor the moment of the Lord's coming makes him prayerful and faithful.

Discovering His Will

One instance wherein humans deeply experience the absence of a manifested Master is when we face important decisions, such as when discerning our vocation in life. We tend to ask for signs, but even in these circumstances, God remains concealed. He will not cease to be an unseen God, for He wants us to discover His will in the advice of reliable persons, in prayer, in self-knowledge, and in the events of daily life. God withdraws from sense perception so that man can exercise freedom in search of the truth.

Why God Hides

Our Freedom

The definitive motive of the Lord's action on our behalf is His love for us. In Sacred Scripture, the Lord manifests Himself not as an anonymous power but as a Person endowed with sentiments, who interacts with His creatures and is in no way indifferent to them.[4]

The hidden God respects the freedom He gave us by not overwhelming us with His overt presence. Because He loves man, the Father shows Himself in the wonders of nature and through Sacred Scripture and Sacred Tradition as authentically interpreted by His Church. He does this, above all, in the person of Jesus Christ, who moved in the midst of people and called them friends.

Vatican II points out that the love of the Maker is shown in His design of creation, salvation, and redemption, and in His inviting us into His company. He wants us to share in His Trinitarian life and happiness. His coming to earth twenty-one centuries ago was not just to visit friends, but because of an ardent desire to make men sharers in His eternal life, adopted sons through the Son, "sons in the Son."

Testing Our Faith

We cannot fully comprehend God's actions, for He has told us, "My thoughts are not your thoughts, neither are your ways my ways" (Isa. 55:8).

St. Peter, the prince of apostles, tells us:

---

[4] See Juan Pablo II, *Cantad al Señor un cántico nuevo*, 162–163.

In this you rejoice, though now for a little while you may have to suffer various trials, so that the genuineness of your faith, more precious than gold which though perishable is tested by fire, may redound to praise and glory and honor at the revelation of Jesus Christ. Without having seen him you love him; though you do not now see him you believe in him and rejoice with unutterable and exalted joy (1 Pet. 1:6–8).

Pope Benedict XVI describes how we can yet glimpse God in His hiddenness:

On one side there is the silence of God and His absence, but in the Resurrection of Christ there is already an anticipation of the "yes" of God; and by this anticipation we live, and through the silence of God, we hear His word; and through the obscurity of His absence we glimpse His light.[5]

The apostles themselves experienced both the presence and the absence of God. Peter, James, and John were flooded with supernatural light during Christ's Transfiguration on Mount Tabor. Conversely, they went through a trial in the Sea of Galilee seemingly without the attention of Jesus:

And behold, there arose a great storm on the sea, so that the boat was being swamped by the waves; but he was asleep. And they went and woke him, saying, "Save, Lord; we are perishing." And he said to them, "Why are you afraid, O men of little faith?" Then he rose and rebuked the winds and the sea; and there was a great calm (Matt. 8:24–26).

---

[5]   Benedict XVI, Homily, June 16, 2012.

When we face such situations, it is possible to think God has abandoned us, but nothing could be further from reality. It is just that our faith is being tested. Such occasions prompted St. Paul to tell the first Christians of Rome: "How unsearchable are his judgments and how inscrutable his ways!" (Rom. 11:33).

Unseen Yet Near

Even though our Lord is invisible — and who has not experienced His silence? — He is not distant. The Triune God dwells in the center of the soul that enjoys His friendship.

He may not be an object of sensorial powers, but He is immanent, living and moving in creation. "God must be invisible to us," observes Cardinal Christoph Schönborn, "so that we do not mistake Him for a bit of the world. The less He manifests Himself in a material way, the more we recognize that He stands opposite the world as its Creator."[6]

There is a barrier between us and the hidden God that we may not cross. Jesus told His disciples, "Where I am going you cannot come" (John 8:21). This is a result of sin, for there was no such impenetrable barrier in Paradise before the Fall. Personal sin weaves a thick veil between creatures and the Almighty and the entire supernatural world.

Yet, although He is hidden from us, God is still near. "If I ascend to heaven," says the psalmist, "thou art there.... If I take the wings of the morning and dwell in the uttermost parts of the sea, even there thy hand shall lead me, and thy right hand shall

[6] Quoted in *Creation and Evolution: A Conference with Pope Benedict XVI*, ed. Stephan Otto Horn and Siegfried Weidenhofer (San Francisco: Ignatius Press, 2008), 129.

hold me" (Ps. 139:8–10). He is omnipresent, particularly in the soul of His children, where He speaks in whispers: Thus, the Lord told Elijah: "'Go forth and stand upon the mount before the LORD.' And behold, the LORD passed by, and a great and strong wind rent the mountains, and broke in pieces the rocks before the LORD, but the LORD was not in the wind; and after the wind an earthquake, but the LORD was not in the earthquake; and after the earthquake a fire, but the LORD was not in the fire; and after the fire a still small voice." (1 Kings 19:11–12).

St. Josemaría Escrivá, the founder of Opus Dei, affirmed:

> The God of our faith is not a distant being who contemplates indifferently the fate of men: their desires, their struggles, and their sufferings. He is a Father who loves His children so much that He sends the Word, the Second Person of the most Blessed Trinity, so that by taking on the nature of man He may die to redeem us. He is the loving Father who now leads us gently to Himself, through the action of the Holy Spirit who dwells in our hearts.[7]

The tendency to be distracted with many earthly concerns and the belief that life is managed entirely by oneself do not correspond with reality. The Lord visits, but only in disguise. He is there, silently waiting for a response. He is to be found in every person, in every event. St. Augustine reminds us that we need not search far for God: "Behold, Thou wert within, and I abroad, and there I searched Thee.... Thou wert with me, but I was not with Thee."[8]

---

[7] Josemaría Escrivá, *Christ Is Passing By* (Manila: Sinag-tala, 1973), no. 131.

[8] St. Augustine, *Confessions* (New York: Book-of-the-Month Club, 1996), 249.

Why God Hides

The future Benedict XVI described our present situation in relation to God in these words:

> Life shared with God, eternal life within temporal life, is possible because of God living with us: Christ is God being here with us. In Him God has time for us; He is God's time for us and thus at the same time the opening of time into eternity. God is no longer the distant and indeterminate God to whom no bridge will reach; He is the God at hand; the body of the Son is the bridge for our souls.... God is no longer merely a God up there, but God surrounds us from above, from below, and from within: He is all in all.[9]

Moreover:

> The healing miracles that Christ performs in the gospel demonstrate that God has drawn near to humanity. With this, Jesus wants to reveal the countenance of the true God, the God who is near, full of mercy for every human being, the God who makes a gift to us of life in abundance, of his own life.[10]

Consequently, the Christian's relationship with the great Lover is something very personal. He is a living God, the Risen Christ, who is also one's best friend: "I have called you friends" (John 15:15). In addition, He is Father, Savior, Advocate, and Lover, who, even when He is ignored, approaches from Heaven with the invitation "Come to me, all you who labor and are heavy laden, and I will give you rest" (Matt. 11:28).

---

[9] Joseph Cardinal Ratzinger, *God Is Near Us* (San Francisco: Ignatius Press, 2003), 144.

[10] Benedict XVI, Angelus, January 27, 2008.

2

The Veils of God

Hide not thy face from me!
—Psalm 143:7

Depending on the point of view, the hidden Lord may appear in a variety of ways: as a merciful Father, a great lover, an epic redeemer, a heroic Savior, a strict judge, a keen observer, an alert proctor, a powerful creator, a wonderful artist, an amazing designer, a splendid giver of grace, a pitiful beggar of faith, a skillful avenger, a master fugitive, perhaps even a stern policeman. This last one is sometimes exemplified in a sign at the back of public vehicles in the Philippines: "God is watching!"

Dietrich von Hildebrand cites the role of fear—filial fear—in trying to know God: "Do not the words of St. Peter after the miraculous catch of fish, 'Depart from me, O Lord, because I am a sinner,' testify that when the reality of God breaks in upon us, we are struck with fear and reverence?"[11] Cardinal Newman

---

[11] Dietrich von Hildebrand, "The Case for the Latin Mass," *Triumph* (October 1966).

showed in a sermon that the man who does not fear and revere has not known the reality of the Almighty.

St. Josemaría Escrivá, for his part, was delighted that God is a most loving Father even if He is not a manifested one. Blessed Cardinal John Henry Newman elaborates on our filial relationship to God:

> [The Christian] addresses God as a child might address his father, with a clear view of Him, and with unmixed confidence; with deep reverence indeed, and godly fear and awe, but still with certainty and exactness (St. Paul wrote, "I know whom I have believed"), with the prospect of judgment to come to sober him, and the assurance of present grace to cheer him.[12]

St. John Paul II likened the Lord to someone who "is ever paying attention to what happens to His favorite creature. God is desirous that in man would shine forever the divine image, in such a way that he would be in the world a sign of harmony, light and peace."[13] He continued:

> He works in human history although He does not operate on the first plane. He works, so to speak, "behind the scenes," respecting the freedom of His creature, but holding in His hands all the world's happenings. The certitude of the providential action of the Maker is a source of hope for the believer who knows that he can

[12] John Henry Newman, *Parochial and Plain Sermons* (San Francisco: Ignatius Press, 1987), 266.

[13] Juan Pablo II, *Laudes con el Papa: Las catequesis de Juan Pablo II sobre los salmos y cánticos de Laudes* (Madrid: Biblioteca de Autores Cristianos, 2003), 262.

count on the constant presence of the One Who "formed the earth, made it, and established it" (Isa. 45:18).[14]

In a homily, Pope Benedict XVI explained the attitude of the withdrawn Lover toward us:

> God gives Himself to us; He does not give something, He gives Himself. And this is not something that happens only at the moment of our conversion. God continues being always the one who gives. He offers us His gifts continuously. He precedes us always.[15]

The veil of the tabernacle symbolizes His veiled presence, and we accordingly cover the tabernacles and the ciboria where the Eucharistic Lord is kept. He is the veiled Someone who loves and seeks love.

We could also view the Lord as someone who complains, saying: Why do you treat me this way? Did I not give you sufficient proof of my love? Why do you treat me as a tough policeman, a slave driver, or a harsh sergeant?

For all believers in Christ, He is someone beyond the eyes of flesh, someone who has been hidden for more than twenty centuries and who will be hidden until the end of time. Yet He is everywhere, and present in prayer, especially when two or more are gathered in His name. Above all, He is present in the sacraments, above all in the Holy Sacrifice of the Mass, in the Eucharist, as well as in all works of mercy for our fellow men, in whose faces we discover him.

---

[14] Ibid., 58.
[15] Benedict XVI, Homily, March 20, 2008.

He appears in different ways, depending on one's perspective. But in all instances, He is real—nay, the source of all reality. Sometimes He seems to be wordless, aloof, distant, powerless, deaf, and even indifferent to our problems and difficulties. But this is a huge wonder, for He is none of these things!

"The LORD," the psalmist tells us, "looks down from heaven, he sees all the sons of men; from where he sits enthroned he looks forth on all the inhabitants of the earth, he who fashions the hearts of them all, and observes all their deeds" (Ps. 33:13–15).

The Lord—it should not be forgotten—not only looks at us but does so with eyes full of paternal affection, much in the way that, as St. Mark testifies, He set His eyes upon the young man who had been leaving a clean life: "And Jesus looking upon him loved him" (Mark 10:21).

How God Is Found

The First Vatican Council stated in *Dei Filius* that "God can be known with certainty from the things that were created, through the natural light of human reason."[16] Hence, the existence and attributes of the Creator can be discovered from created things. This does not mean, however, that we can discover God in the same way we discover the objects of our sense perception, for He remains concealed to our senses.

The second-century *Letter to Diognetus* tells us that God "showed himself by faith only to whomever it was granted to see God" (8:5). This refers to the knowledge of the Lord from

---

[16] First Vatican Council, Dogmatic Constitution on the Catholic Faith *Dei Filius* (April 24, 1870), no. 113.

revelation, the great endowment of God that is to be received with the free response of faith aided by His help.

Belief in revelation freely received makes faith meritorious, for revelation is not made known through sensibly compelling evidence. Faith is a gift that God grants to all who sincerely search for Him, and without faith one cannot please God. It is a requisite for salvation; and since salvation is for all, and since God is goodness itself, He does not deny the gift of faith to anyone who searches for the truth with goodwill. Obviously, the hidden God may manifest Himself in varied extraordinary forms to whomsoever He wants — through mystical experiences such as visions, ecstasies, locutions, and so forth. In these supernatural occurrences, the Lord remains somewhat veiled; the beneficiaries of these occurrences, although deeply affected and enlightened, are not overwhelmed to the point of losing their freedom and their merit.

Seeing God in Calamities

Calamities occur on planet Earth — typhoons, floods, earthquakes, fires, tsunamis, epidemics, and so forth. In such calamities, the Maker can seem to be nowhere in sight.

The large number of disaster victims makes a big impression in our minds, yet the number pales when compared with the some 154,000 persons who die of common causes every day all over the world. Many of them undergo long and painful agony. Dying under extraordinary circumstances and dying of common causes are part of the mortal condition of mankind, proper to people who were expelled from Paradise.

In the case of calamities, they could be caused by a lack of attention to early warnings, denuded mountains, poor meteorological forecasting, lack of preparedness, and other faults of man, but why does the Almighty permit them? This query is more pressing when innocent people such as children are affected. We do not understand. It is mysterious.

The tsunami at the end of 2004 that devastated many Asian and African coasts prompted an American writer to ask, "Where was God?" A Filipino bishop wrote in a newspaper column:

> On December 26, while we were still relishing the joys and pleasures of Christmas, news of an 8.9 magnitude earthquake, off the coast of the Indonesian island of Sumatra, reached us via television. At first there was talk of 23,000 deaths; then the number climbed until it reached 285,993. The TV screens relentlessly showed us pictures of devastated places, and of the broken faces of people who had lost not only their homes and belongings, but their loved ones. The tsunami did not choose its victims. It respected no color or moral qualities. Surely not all those who perished were sinners, and not all were saints either. It struck indiscriminately, with stunning force.
>
> But surely, behind all these sufferings, tragedy, and death was God. It seems as if this time we have no human culprits to blame. That recent mega-tragedy does not call in question the existence of God, but it should make us pause and reflect.
>
> The death of Christ was the worst evil in history because it was the murder of the God-Man, the Second Person of the Blessed Trinity. Now, if God could allow the killing of his own Son, then he could allow anything: the Holocaust, Nagasaki, Hiroshima, and the two world wars. He could allow the killing of millions under Stalin and Mao, and the recent genocide of 800,000 in Rwanda. He could allow

abortion of 50,000,000 babies every year, and now the unexpected death of 285,993 humans from the tsunami.

What God cannot allow is for suffering, death, and evil to have the last word. He can allow the worst that man and nature can do, provided that the last word is His. And this word will be words of love and life.

We see and not only hear this word of God: in the unprecedented generosity with which the world raised more than $5,000,000,000 for the victims of the tsunami, in response to the appeal of the Pope and bishops for prayers and help; from volunteer-workers and holiday-makers who, on escaping death, stayed to help the hapless victims. God speaks His word of love in the erasure of the boundaries and distinctions among people. Suddenly, we are just one human family, setting aside differences and enmities, and sharing one another's burdens. Hong Kong and Singapore deliberately muted their New Year celebrations to express solidarity with the sufferers. This terrible tragedy brought about a new sense of a great, single human family.

How true the words by St. Paul: "We know that God makes everything work for good for those who love God" (Rom. 8:28). And how correct the great St. Augustine was when he wrote: "[The Lord] would not in His goodness allow anything to happen were he not able in His omnipotence to bring good even out of evil" (*The Enchiridion on Faith, Hope, and Love*). The Lord has indeed made the best of humanity come out in this worst of calamities. Love still emerges triumphant![17]

---

[17] Bishop Teodoro Bacani, *Manila Standard Today*, December 30, 2004.

Why God Hides

Calamities make us realize our precarious condition on earth, that we do not have a permanent abode here, and that the Almighty could call an end to our terrestrial existence without notice. These events make us realize our dependence on the Almighty, that we do not "run the show," that He does, and that everything and everyone is in His hands.

Adversities remind us that we are in exile and traveling toward our Fatherland. They awaken us from the torpor of a false security. Our good planet was affected by sin, although sanctified and consecrated by Jesus Christ. Disasters are repercussions of sin (in Paradise there were no calamities), as well as stern reminders that something went wrong at the beginning and continues to go wrong throughout mankind's history.

We might not understand why things such as tsunamis happen, but when such misfortunes strike, we must bow our heads in acceptance of God's will: "Your will be done! No matter what it is!" One day the end of the world will come. What man can do is to be prepared at all times, to say yes to God.

As for the question "Could a just God permit this disaster?" the answer is that God owes us nothing; all we have originates from Him. He gives, and He takes back; He has all the rights over us, and we have none over Him. The Almighty does not have to reward or to punish us in this brief life on earth. He has the whole of eternity to exercise retribution. His last word does not have to be uttered now. The Lord is not constrained to mete out justice in this life. Sometimes He exacts repayment immediately, other times in the next world, and sometimes partly now and partly later.

This matter is entirely up to God! That is why the whole idea of *karma* is untenable. It is pretentious, for it amounts to claiming that we know something that only the Supreme Being knows.

At the origin of all evils is the evil of sin, which converted "our exile" into a "valley of tears." There were no earthquakes, no floods, no tsunamis, and no epidemics in Eden, and there are many things on earth that remind us of the original Paradise: the joy of loving and being loved, flowers, colorful birds and fish, stars, sunsets, rainbows, and waterfalls.

Says Alfonso Aguiló:

It does not seem serious to blame God for all that does not go well in this world. "Are the human beings," wrote C. S. Lewis, "the ones who have produced the instruments of torture, whips, slavery, cannons, bayonets and bombs? It is due to human greediness or stupidity and not to the absence of natural resources that we suffer poverty." In many of these complaints that some people throw at God, there is a regrettable confusion. They consider God as a strange individual on whom they load the obligation of solving all that we have done wrong.[18]

Who caused the terrible alteration from happy people in Paradise to exiled persons on earth? Not God but Adam, Eve, Cain, and all sinners. St. Josemaría Escrivá wrote: "This world was beautiful when it came out of God's hands; we have made it ugly with our sins,"[19] an allusion to the cosmic repercussions of human sin to which St. Paul referred when he wrote:

We know that the whole creation has been groaning in travail together until now; and not only the creation, but

---

[18] Alfonso Aguiló, *Es razonable creer?* (Madrid: Ediciones Palabra, 2009), 69.

[19] See *Conversations with Monsignor Escrivá de Balaguer* (Manila: Sinag-tala, 1985), no. 70.

we ourselves, who have the first fruits of the Spirit, groan inwardly as we wait for adoption as sons, the redemption of our bodies (Rom. 8:22–23).

In the economy of salvation, the hope of deliverance and recovery of the lost Paradise are based on the merits of Jesus Christ, who opened the gates of Heaven for us, and so now, we look forward to the announced "new heavens and new earth" (2 Pet. 3:13).

A good effect of calamities is the awakening in hearts of a keen desire for a different and better world, where there would be no tears, no suffering, and no death. The disgust for our present condition should give way to an eagerness to enjoy the happiness of Heaven, our Father's house, our original destination. "I send people troubles in this world," Jesus told St. Catherine of Siena, so that they may know that their goal is not this life, and that these things are imperfect and passing. I am their goal, and I want them to want me, and in this spirit they should accept such things."[20]

Sufferings from calamities provide occasions for God's children to share in the redemptive sufferings of Christ. They constitute an opportunity to expiate, co-redeem, and participate in the saving Cross of our Lord. How well the great saint of Avila, St. Teresa of Jesus, understood this when she wrote that famous maxim: "Sisters, she who can suffer more, let her suffer, and she will come out the better off!"[21]

---

[20] St. Catherine of Siena, *The Dialogue* (London: Kegan Paul, Trench, Trubner, 1907), no. 49.

[21] *Hermanas, la que pueda sufrir más, que sufra, y saldrá la mejor Librada.*

"All Things Work Together unto Good"

For St. Josemaría Escrivá, to trust in God means to have faith, no matter what happens. The eternal Lover is behind every event, though at times in a manner incomprehensible to us. St. Josemaría insisted that things are not as we want them to be, but the way that God, in His providence, wants or allows them to be. Hence, we have to accept them gladly, no matter how they appear. If we know how to see God behind everything that happens, we will always be happy and peaceful and never get distressed.

Jacques Philippe explains that faith tells us how God is good and powerful enough to use in our favor all the evil and suffering in the world. Evil is a mystery and a scandal. Its place in the economy of redemption belongs to the Lord's wisdom, however, not to our understanding of things: "For my thoughts are not your thoughts, neither are your ways my ways, says the LORD. For as the heavens are higher than the earth, so are my ways higher than your ways" (Isa. 55:8–9).

Furthermore, we have the certitude that "the sufferings of this present time are not worth comparing with the glory that is to be revealed to us" and that "all things work together unto good for those who love God" (see Rom. 8:18, 28). As Peter Kreeft says that, for those who take a "'leap of faith' all things work together for good, because once we leap into God's will, we leap into pure goodness."[22]

It is in the face of natural calamities that trust in the divine goodness is most challenged; even God's very existence might be put into question, prompting us to ask, "Is He there?" This

---

[22] Peter Kreeft, *How to Be Holy: First Steps in Becoming a Saint* (San Francisco: Ignatius Press, 2016), p. 27.

is the attitude of someone who, in the middle of the night, asks if the sun exists. It is in these dark hours that great merits can be earned, if faith and trust in the concealed Father are upheld.

Pope John Paul II referred to this when he commented on Isaiah 42:

> When God seems to be silent amid oppression, injustice, and suffering, He still loves human beings and comes to their aid when invoked. It might seem to the believer, especially if he bears the weight of a painful experience, that God is silent. Even the great mystical saints experienced this state, which St. John of the Cross called the "dark night of the soul." The prophet Isaiah teaches us that whoever believes with confidence, despite everything, that God is near and acts, will survive the time of trial and will give thanks to God with joy for his constant love which delivers from all evil. God's silence does not indicate absence.

Pope John Paul II ended by quoting Romano Guardini, who said that "the earth is pervaded by a cosmic ecstasy. There is in it an eternal reality and presence that must now reveal itself, as in an epiphany of God, through all that exists."[23]

On May 28, 2006, Benedict XVI visited the Auschwitz concentration camp, where he said:

> To speak in this place of horror, in this place where unprecedented mass crimes were committed against God and man, is almost impossible.... In a place like this, words fail.... In the end, there can only be a dread silence—a

---

[23] John Paul II, General Audience, April 2, 2003.

silence which is itself a heartfelt cry to God: Why, Lord, did you remain silent? How could you tolerate all this?... Where was God in those days? Why was he silent? .... We cannot peer into God's mysterious plan—we see only piecemeal, and we would be wrong to set ourselves up as judges of God and history.

While acknowledging that we do not understand God, Benedict XVI pointed out that the Almighty has a more comprehensive view of reality.

3

How God Reveals Himself

The invisible Friend chooses to help us in our search for Him in many ways and times, and one such way is through *revelation*, which means removing the veil a bit. The greatest manifestation of God to mankind occurred when the Word was made flesh in the womb of Mary Immaculate and dwelt among us.

In the book of Genesis, Jacob, after wrestling with a mysterious person, "called the name of the place Peniel, saying, 'For I have seen God face to face, and yet my life is preserved'" (Gen. 32:30).

In the book of Jeremiah, we read that, "in the beginning of the reign of Zedekiah the son of Josiah, king of Judah, this word came from the LORD" (26:1). "This word" was a message from Yahweh about man's redemption.

In the Acts of the Apostles, when the first Christian martyr, St. Stephen, was being stoned to death, he said, "Behold, I see the heavens opened, and the Son of man standing at the right hand of God" (Acts 7:56). Is it not the aspiration of everyone to see the heavens open before us?

St. Paul tells us about some of the revelations he experienced: "I know a man in Christ who, fourteen years ago, was caught up to the third heaven—whether in the body or out of the body I do not know; God knows.... And he heard things that cannot be told, which man may not utter" (2 Cor. 12:2, 4).

Throughout the history of the Catholic Church there have been a good number of accounts from dependable sources—side by side with unreliable ones that merit no credence—that show how the silent Lover has occasionally broken His silence and manifested Himself. He has done so for a few friends who were made privy to His secrets. They were among the most privileged people on earth, for they were given a wisdom that eclipses human knowledge. It would be good, however, to ponder a well-known saying of St. Josemaría, who was a recipient of such favors: "I do not wish them for anybody, for they carry enormous demands."[24]

St. Thomas Aquinas had a mystical experience after which he did not wish to continue writing the *Summa Theologiae*. After an undescribed revelation while celebrating Mass, he said: "The end of my labors is come. All that I have written appears to me to be as so much straw after the things that have been revealed to me."[25]

Many saints, including St. Teresa of Jesus, St. John of the Cross, and St. Josemaría Escrivá, experienced a multitude of extraordinary favors in the form of visions, ecstasies, and locutions.

Manuel García Morente (1886–1942) taught philosophy at the University of Madrid. In 1937, as he listened on the radio to *L'énfance de Jesus* from Berlioz, he experienced a deep peace:

Through my mind childhood images of Jesus Christ started marching. That event had a fulminating effect on

---

[24] *No las deseo para nadie pues son de una enorme exigencia.*

[25] Kristin E. White, *A Guide to the Saints* (New York: Ivy Books, 1991), 361.

my soul. [He started praying "Your will be done on earth as it is in heaven." All of a sudden, something extraordinary happened.] He was there. I did not see Him. I did not hear Him. I did not touch Him. But He was there. I perceived Him, albeit without sensations.[26]

The following day he decided to embrace the priestly state. He was ordained a priest in 1940.

André Frossard, a member of the French Academy, was one of the most influential intellectuals of his time. His father was a communist, and André was raised in an atmosphere of atheism and laicism. He wrote a book entitled *God Exists, I Met Him*, in which he recounts an experience when he was twenty years old:

> Having entered, at 5:10 p.m., a chapel of the Latin District of Paris, looking for a friend of mine, I came out at 5:15 with a companion who was not of this earth. After entering the place skeptical and atheistic ... indifferent and busy with things very different from a God whom I did not even have the intention of denying ... I came out a few minutes later, catholic, apostolic, and Roman, carried, lifted, collected, and swept by the wave of an inexhaustible joy![27]

André Frossard died in 1994, at age eighty, after giving sterling witness to his Faith from that decisive moment of his conversion.

---

[26] See Martin Velasco, "La conversión de Manuel García Morente," *Augustinus* 32, nos. 125–128 (1987): 475–497.

[27] André Frossard, *Dios existe, yo me lo encontré* (Madrid: Ediciones Rialp, 2002), 37.

Miracles

The veil is thin when God manifests Himself in various periods of history through miracles. They are extraordinary events that show in time and space God's power and glory, disclosures that build up faith and bring about salvation. Those occasions in which a miracle restores health or even life show God's goodness and benevolence.[28]

We read of many miracles in the Gospels and the Acts of the Apostles. Why do they seem so rare now? St. Gregory the Great, who lived in the sixth century, explained: "These signs were needed in the beginning, but not in later years when faith had become rooted in the world. Then, the Church itself became the principal sign of God among men."[29]

Miracles have been reported in great numbers throughout history. As part of her mission, the Church distinguishes the authentic from the fake. Dr. Francis Collins, one of the world's renowned scientists, affirms:

> Miracles do not pose an irreconcilable conflict for the believer who trusts in science as a means to investigate the natural world, and who sees that the natural world is ruled by laws. If, like me, you admit that there might exist something or someone outside of nature, then there is no logical reason why that force could not on rare occasions stage an invasion.[30]

---

[28] See OSV's *Catholic Encyclopedia* (Huntington, Indiana: Our Sunday Visitor, 1991), 645.

[29] St. Gregory the Great, *Homiliae in Evangelia* 29.4.

[30] Francis S. Collins, *The Language of God* (New York: Free Press, 2006), 53.

Among the most famous of miracles is Mary's apparition to St. Bernadette Soubirous in Lourdes, France. In 1882, a medical bureau was established to test the authenticity of the cures that followed the apparitions. Today, the bureau acts as a "first-instance tribunal," which sends its findings to the International Medical Committee of Lourdes for a final verdict. This committee is under medical, not ecclesiastical, supervision. Thousands of people have sought to have their cases confirmed as miracles, but only a few cases have been declared scientifically inexplicable.

In his book *The Voyage to Lourdes*, Alexis Carrel, a Nobel laureate in medicine, tells the story of a young woman, Mary Baille, who was dying of tubercular peritonitis. Her sudden cure took place in Lourdes on May 28, 1902, under Carrel's skeptical eyes. The gift of faith came to Carrel after many years, following his spellbinding experience in Lourdes.[31]

The Church follows certain processes for the beatification and canonization of saints. Except for the case of martyrs, two miracles obtained through the intercession of the candidate are usually required, one for beatification, and one for canonization. The Church will always be most careful in certifying miracles and will not be overawed just because the doctor who states that medical science cannot explain the healing happens to be a Nobel laureate.[32] The Church shows extreme carefulness, because in doing so she simply cares for that supernatural vitality of hers, of which miracles are the most palpable signs.[33]

---

[31] Alexis Carrel, *The Voyage to Lourdes* (Port Huron, Michigan: Real-View Books, 2006), introduction.

[32] The Church did not certify as a miracle the cure that greatly impressed Alexis Carrel.

[33] Address by Rev. Stanley L. Jaki at the 67th Annual Convention of Catholic Medical Doctors, September 13, 1998.

Why God Hides

The Miracle of the Sun occurred in Fatima on October 13, 1917. On October 15, 1917, the secular newspaper O *Seculo* printed on its front page, "COMO O SOL BAILOU AD MEDIO DIA EM FATIMA" (How the sun danced at midday in Fatima). Msgr. William C. McGrath, who studied the event, gave a description:

> Gradually the sun grew pale, lost its normal color, and appeared as a silver disk at which all could gaze directly without even shading their eyes.... Then, while the crowd went on its knees in abject terror, the sun suddenly seemed to be torn loose from its place in the heavens ... as it zigzagged through the skies while from all parts of the now terrified multitude arose cries of repentance and appeals for mercy.... Suddenly, as if arrested in its downward plunge by an invisible heavenly hand, it paused for a moment and then, in the same series of swirling motions it began to climb upward till it resumed its accustomed place in the heavens. Gone was the silver disk with the brilliant rays. It was once more a ball of fire at which nobody could look with unshaded eyes.
>
> While people looked at one another, still trembling from their terrifying experience and not yet sure that some further disaster would overtake them, a cry of astonishment was heard on every side. Their rain-sodden garments had suddenly dried.[34]

There were about seventy thousand people gathered on that occasion, persons of all walks of life, mostly inhabitants of the

---

[34] Msgr. William C. McGrath, in John J. Delaney, A *Woman Clothed with the Sun: The Lady of the Rosary* (Manila: Sinagtala, 1988), 202.

neighboring areas, many of them skeptical and unbelieving. What was clear was that it was a supernatural event and a great miracle.

Sister Lúcia related how the Virgin Mary told her on the previous July 13 and on September 13 that a sign would be given on October 13. On September 13, 1917, Sister Lúcia told Our Lady, "They have asked me to ask you many things, the cure of some sick persons, of a deaf mute." "Yes," Our Lady answered, "I will cure some, others no. In October, I will work a miracle so that all will believe."[35]

Pope Pius XII, who declared the Assumption of Our Lady a dogma, revealed in a handwritten note that he had seen the miracle of the sun four times from the Vatican gardens. He wrote: "I have seen the 'miracle of the sun,' this is the pure truth."[36] Since his experience of the phenomenon happened on November 1, 1950, when the Pope proclaimed the dogma of the Assumption, it seems to be a supernatural confirmation of the dogma.

Prophecy

Through prophecy, the Almighty has granted some persons to know events in advance. These may be supernatural occurrences in which the concealed Father removes the veil for the edification and consolation of souls. The instances of prophecy recorded in Sacred Scripture are numerous. The messianic prophecies — such as those of the prophet Isaiah — were fulfilled with the coming of

[35] Lúcia de Jesus, *Memorias de Lúcia: La vidente de Fatima*, 3rd ed. (Madrid: Ediciones "Sol de Fátima," 1980), 151.

[36] Antonio Gaspari, "Pius XII Saw 'Miracle of the Sun,'" Zenit, November 4, 2008, https://zenit.org/articles/pius-xii-saw-miracle-of-the-sun/.

Jesus Christ. Together with prophecy, the miracles accompanying revelation, which is the supernatural manifestation of concealed truths for the good of the Church, lend credibility to revelation.

Reginald Garrigou-Lagrange explains this phenomenon in these terms:

> Down the centuries, as a manifestation of the power of the Holy Spirit, there have been documented occasions in which prophecies have been made of future events and they have occurred as predicted. They, besides, have happened in such a way that they show a supernatural intervention, a disclosure on the part of God. Nonetheless, they are private revelations that, no matter how much importance they have, do not belong, to the deposit of Catholic faith.[37]

A modern instance of prophecy is that of St. Anthony Mary Claret, who, in 1859, wrote:

> On September 23 at 7:30 in the morning, the Lord gave me to know great things about the words of the Apocalypse: "And I saw and heard the voice of an eagle" (Rev. 8:13) which flew through the middle of the sky and said with loud and emphatic voice: "Woe, woe to the inhabitants of the earth because of the three great punishments that are to come, which are first, communism; second, the four archdemons which promote in a terrible way the love of pleasures, the love of money, autonomy of thought, and self-will; and third, great wars and their consequences."[38]

[37] Reginald Garrigou-Lagrange, *The Three Ages of the Interior Life*, vol. 2. (Rockford, IL: TAN, 1989), 580.

[38] Daniel Sargent, *The Assignments of Antonio Claret* (New York: Declan X. McMullen, 1948), 143.

In the light of the historical events that occurred afterward, these predictions made in 1859 constitute an imposing disclosure of the veiled Lord.

Early in the twentieth century, Our Lady made a number of prophecies to the little shepherds of Fatima concerning events that subsequently came to pass. On October 13, 1917, Our Lady told the children at the Cova da Iria: "Continue praying the Rosary daily. The war is coming to an end and the soldiers will come back to their homes soon."[39] The First World War started in 1914 and ended on November 11, 1918.

On June 13, 1917, Lucia asked Our Lady to take the three little shepherds to Heaven. Her reply: "Certainly, I will take Jacinta and Francisco soon. But you must stay here longer." Francisco died on April 4, 1919, and less than two years later, Jacinta died on February 20, 1920. In accordance with Our Lady's prediction, Lucia "stayed longer" and died on February 13, 2005, at age ninety-seven.

The predictions made by Our Lady at Cova da Iria on June 13, 1917, included the following:

> You saw hell where the souls of the poor sinners go. To save them God wants to establish in the world devotion to my Immaculate Heart. If they do what I tell you, many souls will be saved, and they will have peace. This war is coming to an end, but if they do not stop offending God … another war, worse than this one, will begin.
>
> When you see a night illuminated by a strange light, you will know this is the sign God gives you that He is

---

[39] See P. Fernando Leite, *The Apparitions of Fatima*, 3rd ed. (Sec. Nacional do Apostolado), 20.

going to punish the world for its crimes with war, famine, and persecutions of the Church and the Pope. To prevent this, I will come to beg the consecration of Russia to my Immaculate Heart and Communion in atonement on the first Saturday of each month. If my requests are heeded, Russia will be converted, and they will have peace; if not, Russia will spread errors over the world, provoking wars, and persecutions of the Church; the faithful will suffer martyrdom; the Pope will suffer greatly, and a number of countries will disappear. Eventually, my Immaculate Heart will triumph. The Pope will consecrate Russia to my Immaculate Heart; she will be converted, and the world will have some time of peace.[40]

Fernando Leite comments:

Everything Our Lady foretold in this apparition happened: the devotion in atonement for sin on the first Saturdays was asked by Our Lady at three successive apparitions.... Our Lady requested the consecration of Russia to her Immaculate Heart....

When sin prevented the carrying out of these requests at the right time, an *aurora borealis*, the sign of terrible punishment, lit up the night of January 25 to 26, 1938. On the 1st of September 1939, the Second World War began. During that six-year war, millions of lives were lost, towns and countries were ruined. Russia spread her errors all over the world, provoking wars and persecutions against the Church. Many Christians endured martyrdom, and the Pope was tormented by distress and anguish. A number of

---

[40] Delaney, *A Woman Clothed with the Sun*, 211.

countries were destroyed or lost their independence. Pius XII consecrated the world, with special mention of Russia, to the Immaculate Heart of Mary on October 31, 1942. On March 25, 1984, Pope John Paul II consecrated the world together with "those men and nations that stand more in need of this offering and this consecration."[41]

Soon after, great changes began in Europe from one country that had been dominated by the communist Soviet Union to another. The fall of communism in Eastern Europe was symbolized by the fall of the Berlin Wall in 1989. To signify the relationship between the apparitions of Fatima and the collapse of communism, a piece of the Berlin wall is kept on display in the Chapel of Our Lady in Fatima.

Another modern-age prophecy concerns the third secret of Fatima. The following is a translation of the original Portuguese text of this secret, revealed to the three shepherd children at the Cova da Iria, Fatima, on July 13, 1917, and submitted in writing by Sister Lucia on January 3, 1944:

> I write in obedience to you, my God, who commands me to do so through his Excellency the Bishop of Leiria and through your Most Holy Mother and mine.
>
> After the two parts which I have already explained, at the left of Our Lady and a little above, we saw an angel with a flaming sword in his left hand flashing; it gave out flames that looked as though they would set the world on fire. But they died out in contact with the splendor that Our Lady radiated towards him from her right hand. Pointing to the earth with his right hand,

[41] Leite, *The Apparitions of Fatima*, 13–14.

the angel cried out in a loud voice, "Penance, Penance, Penance!" And we saw in an immense light that is God, "something similar to how people appear in a mirror when they pass in front of it," a Bishop dressed in white. "We had the impression that it was the Holy Father," other bishops, priests, men and women Religious going up a steep mountain, at the top of which was a big Cross of rough-hewn trunks as of a cork-tree with the bark. Before reaching there the Holy Father passed through a big city half in ruins, and half trembling with halting step, afflicted with pain and sorrow, he prayed for the souls of the corpses he met on his way. Having reached the top of the mountain, on his knees at the foot of the big Cross, he was killed by a group of soldiers who fired bullets and arrows at him, and in the same way, there died one after another the other bishops, priests, men and women Religious, and various lay people of different ranks and positions. Beneath the two arms of the Cross, there were two angels, each with a crystal aspersorium in his hand, in which they gathered up the blood of the martyrs, and with it sprinkled the souls that were making their way to God.[42]

An authoritative interpretation of this document was read by Cardinal Angelo Sodano, secretary of state of Pope John Paul II, on May 13, 2000:

---

[42] Congregation for the Doctrine of the Faith, *The Message of Fatima*, "Third Part of the 'Secret,'" http://www.vatican.va/ roman_curia/congregations/cfaith/documents/rc_con_ cfaith_doc_20000626_message-fatima_en.html.

That text contains a prophetic vision similar to those found in Sacred Scripture, which do not describe with photographic clarity the details of future events, but rather synthesize and condense against a unified background events spread out over time in a succession and duration which are not specified. As a result, the text must be interpreted in a symbolic key.

The vision of Fatima concerns above all the war waged by atheist systems against the Church and Christians, and it describes the immense suffering endured by the witnesses of faith in the last century of the second millennium. It is an interminable Way of the Cross led by the Popes of the twentieth century.

According to the interpretation of the "little shepherds" which was also confirmed by Sister Lucia, the "Bishop clothed in white" who prays for all the faithful is the Pope.[43]

After the assassination attempt on Pope John Paul II on May 13, 1981, it was evident to His Holiness that it was a motherly hand that guided the bullet's path. At the behest of the bishop of Leiria, Fatima, the bullet that had remained in the jeep was donated to the Fatima shrine by Pope John Paul II and was later set in the crown of the statue of Our Lady of Fatima.

Successive events in 1989 led to the fall of the Soviet Union and a number of other countries of Eastern Europe. For this, too, His Holiness offered heartfelt thanks to the Most Holy Virgin.

In other parts of the world, attacks against the Church and against Christians continue. Even if the events to which the

---

[43] Ibid., "Announcement Made by Cardinal Angelo Sodano, Secretary of State."

third part of the secret of Fatima refers are now past, Our Lady's call to conversion and penance remains timely and urgent today.

On June 13, 1994, Pope John Paul II addressed the College of Cardinals and said:

> It was given to me, personally, to understand in a particular manner the message of Fatima: the first time, the 13th of May 1981, in the moment of the attempt against the life of the Pope; later, towards the end of the eighties, on the occasion of the defeat of communism in the countries of the soviet bloc. I think that it was an experience quite transparent for everyone.[44]

The historian John Coverdale, in narrating the early years of Opus Dei (1928–1943), mentions an event that shows the vision of the future that, on occasion, God had granted to St. Josemaría. It is an account that it is as impressive as it is painful. In his excellent book *Uncommon Faith*, Coverdale states:

> Towards the end of July 1938, Escrivá received disturbing news from a friend. A high-ranking treasury official, who was an old rival of Casciaro's[45] father in provincial politics, was preparing to denounce Casciaro as a Communist who had crossed the lines as a spy and was now in a sensitive position in the code section of army headquarters. Casciaro went with Miguel Fisac, who was in Burgos at the time, to see if they could persuade the official's

---

[44] *L'Osservatore Romano* (English ed.), June 24, 1994.

[45] Pedro Casciaro was one of the first members of Opus Dei. In 1937, he crossed the Pyrenees with St. Josemaría and was living in Burgos with him.

wife to convince her husband that the accusations were groundless. Their visit was unsuccessful.

On the morning of August 1, 1938, Escrivá went with Albareda to visit the official. The appeals to justice and compassion having failed, Escrivá warned him of the spiritual harm he was inflicting upon himself and that he might have to account to God that very day for his deeds. Escrivá's warnings fell in deaf ears. Referring to Casciaro's father's prominent role in center-left provincial politics and supposed crimes during the war, the official repeated stubbornly, "Both father and son have to pay." Albareda and Escrivá left the office disheartened.

As he walked down the stairs, Escrivá muttered to himself, "Tomorrow or the next day, a funeral." A few hours later, walking through the streets of Burgos, Escrivá noticed a poster on a church wall announcing—as was the custom in Spain during that period—a funeral. The funeral was for the fifty-one-year-old official who had been stricken by a sudden attack and had died in his office that morning, shortly after his meeting with Escrivá and Albareda.

When Casciaro returned to the hotel for lunch, Escrivá related as gently as possible, what had happened. "He said," Casciaro recalls, "he thanked God for His obvious care for me and my father, although the event itself was painful. He also told me not to worry about that man, because he was morally certain God had mercy on him and had granted him final repentance. He said he had not ceased praying for him and his children from the moment he left his office."

"From that day forward," Casciaro adds, "all my life I have prayed for his soul and for his whole family.... God will have rewarded him for all his good works and will no doubt have forgiven him for those moments of darkness so understandable in the chaotic climate of the war."[46]

Stigmata

It is a fact that some persons are given by God an opportunity to share in Christ's Passion in a special manner. They receive marks on their bodies that correspond to the wounds suffered by Jesus in His Crucifixion. Stigmatics bear on their hands, feet, side, or forehead the marks of the Passion of Christ, together with intense sufferings. These are called visible stigmata. Others have the sufferings without the outward marks, and this is called invisible stigmata.

The Church considers about 300 stigmatics as having genuine signs of favor from the Lord. Perhaps the most famous is St. Francis of Assisi, who, in 1224, received on his body the marks of the Lord's Passion, which never healed. In modern times, stigmatics have included Theresa Neumann (1898–1962) of Germany and the Italian Padre Pio, who was proclaimed a saint by Pope John Paul II.

In our time, Padre Pio acquired great fame. Born Francesco Forgione on May 25, 1887, at Pietrelcina in southeastern Italy, Padre Pio joined the Capuchin Order in 1903, was ordained in 1910, and received the sacred wounds of Christ on September 20, 1918. During the fifty-eight years he was a priest, his monastery at San Giovanni Rotondo was visited by thousands of pilgrims from all over the world. Besides the stigmata, which modern medical science cannot explain, Padre Pio possessed other unusual gifts, such as the

---

[46] John F. Coverdale, *Uncommon Faith* (Princeton and New York: Scepter, 2002), 271–272.

reading of hearts, miraculous cures, remarkable conversions, and prophetic insight. He died on September 23, 1968. His funeral was attended by more than one hundred thousand people. Hundreds of thousands worldwide rejoiced when Padre Pio of Pietrelcina was beatified on May 2, 1999 and canonized on June 16, 2002.

What could possibly explain these phenomena? No one has ever shown that imagination can produce wounds in a normal subject.[47] Psychologist Pierre Janet tried for many years to produce stigmata by hypnotic suggestion, without success.[48] Physicians have also been unsuccessful in curing these wounds with medical remedies. "What has been said of the stigmatic wounds applies to the sufferings. There is not a single experimental proof that the imagination can produce them."[49]

It is reasonable to take these phenomena as instances in which the Almighty is less concealed. Garrigou-Lagrange states:

They are exceptional signs given by the Lord, from time to time, to draw us from our spiritual somnolence and to attract our attention more strongly to the great mysteries of faith by which we should live more profoundly every day, in particular to the mystery of the redemptive Incarnation....

Many men and women saints, of widely different temperaments, have been absorbed with ardent love in the infused contemplation of the sufferings of Christ, but they have not had the stigmata. This is a sign that ardent

---

[47] Augustin Poulain, "Mystical Stigmata," *Catholic Encyclopedia*, vol. 14 (New York: Robert Appleton, 1912), http://www.newadvent.org/cathen/14294b.htm.

[48] Garrigou-Lagrange, *The Three Ages of the Interior Life*, 597.

[49] Poulain, "Mystical Stigmata."

love, united to infused contemplation, does not suffice to produce the stigmata. Christ Jesus grants them to whom He will, when He will, and as He will. Stigmatization is an essentially extraordinary grace that is not in the normal way of sanctity.[50]

Supernatural Visions

A vision is the supernatural perception of an object naturally invisible to man. The term "supernatural" is used to distinguish true visions from illusions or hallucinations that proceed from natural causes, as well as the fraudulent visions produced by the devil. Apparitions concerning the divinity should normally be considered, St. Teresa states, as "some kind of representation." They are not presumed to be intuitive or face-to-face visions of the Divine Essence, for these are reserved for the souls in Heaven.[51]

Spiritual writers distinguish among supernatural visions, calling them (1) sensible, when they are detectable by the external senses; (2) imaginary, when produced in the imagination by God or the angels; and (3) intellectual, when the manifestations to the intellect are without dependence on sensible images. Visions require the infused light of wisdom or of prophecy.[52] Thus, St. Teresa often felt our Lord Jesus Christ near her for several days. She wrote about these visions in her autobiography:

There is nothing we can do about them; we cannot see more or less of them at will; and we can neither call them

---

[50] Garrigou-Lagrange, *The Three Ages of the Interior Life*, 579, 604.

[51] Cf. Jordan Aumann, O.P., *Spiritual Theology* (Manila: UST Faculty of Theology, 1989), 425.

[52] Garrigou-Lagrange, *The Three Ages of the Interior Life*, 586.

up nor banish them by our efforts. The Lord's will is that we shall see quite clearly that they are produced, not by us but by His Majesty. Still less can we be proud of them; on the contrary, they make us humble and fearful when we find that just as the Lord takes from us the power to see what we desire, so He can also take from us those favors and His grace, with the result that we are completely lost. So while we live in this exile, let us always walk with fear.

Almost invariably the Lord showed Himself to me in His resurrected body, and it was thus, too, that I saw Him in the host. Only occasionally, to strengthen me when I was in tribulation, did He show me His wounds, and then He would appear sometimes as He was on the cross and sometimes as in the garden. On a few occasions I saw Him wearing the crown of thorns and, sometimes, He would also be carrying the cross—because of my necessities, as I say, and those of others—but always in His glorified flesh. Many are the affronts and trials that I have suffered through telling this, and many are the fears and persecutions that it has brought me. So sure were those to whom I told of it that I had a devil, that some of them wanted to exorcize me. This troubled me very little, but I was sorry when I found that my confessors were afraid to hear my confessions or when I heard that people were saying things to them against me. Nonetheless, I could never regret having seen these heavenly visions and would not exchange them for all the good things and delights of this world.[53]

---

[53] *The Life of Teresa of Jesus: The Autobiography of St. Teresa of Avila* (New York: Doubleday-Image, 1960), 269–270.

Why God Hides

In chapter 27 of her autobiography, she wrote:

> I was at prayer on a festival of the glorious Saint Peter when
> I saw Christ at my side; or, to put it better, I was conscious
> of Him, for neither with the eyes of the body nor with those
> of the soul did I see anything.... All the time Jesus Christ
> seemed to be beside me, but as this was not an imaginary
> vision, I could not discern in what form; what I felt very
> clearly was that all the time He was at my right hand, and
> a witness of everything that I was doing, and that whenever
> I became slightly recollected or was not greatly distracted,
> I could not but be aware of His nearness to me.[54]

A vision experienced by the same saint is the one known
as the Transverberation, of which there is a superb sculptural
rendition in St. Peter's Basilica in Rome. St. Teresa herself wrote
about it:

> It pleased the Lord that I should sometimes see the
> following vision. I would see beside me, on my left hand,
> an angel in bodily form—a type of vision which I am not
> in the habit of seeing, except very rarely. Though I often
> see representations of angels, my visions of them are of
> a type which I first mentioned. It pleased the Lord that
> I should see this angel in the following way. He was not
> tall, but short, and very beautiful, his face so aflame that
> he appeared to be one of the highest types of angel who
> seem to be all afire.... In his hands I saw a long golden
> spear and at the end of the iron tip I seemed to see a point
> of fire. With this he seemed to pierce my heart several

---

[54] Ibid., 249.

times so that it penetrated to my entrails. When he drew it out, I thought he was drawing them out with it and he left me completely afire with great love for God. The pain was so sharp that it made me utter several moans; and so excessive was the sweetness caused me by this intense pain that one can never wish to lose it, nor will one's soul be content with anything else than God. It is not bodily pain, but spiritual, though the body has a share in it — indeed, a great share. So sweet are the colloquies of love which pass between the soul and God that if anyone thinks I am lying I beseech God, in His goodness, to give him the same experience.[55]

By means of visions granted to holy persons, the Lord manifests Himself to humanity. He usually leaves a door open for skeptics to attribute them to hallucinations and other psychological conditions, or even fraud. Many instances are credible on account of the honesty and mental soundness of the author, or because the whole literary context "rings true."

To the latter belongs what happened in the summer of 1921 to Edith Stein, then twenty-nine, who exclaimed: "The truth is here!" She had been visiting with friends but found herself alone for the evening. She looked for a book to read and picked the autobiography of St. Teresa of Avila, which she read in one sitting. There and then, she reached the conclusion that the Catholic Faith was true. She was converted and the following day she bought a catechism and a missal.

With the Lord's help, Edith Stein took the step that went from conjecture to certitude of faith, which she kept to the very

[55] Ibid., 274–275.

end. The future saint could have dismissed the narrations of the visions of St. Teresa as pathological occurrences; instead, she understood that the truth she was looking for was right there; and she believed in the accounts of the saint of Avila as authentic reflections of the truth.

Locutions

Another way in which the concealed Friend manifests Himself is through locutions, which are affirmations or statements supernaturally effected.[56] St. John of the Cross wrote of them:

> When the soul receives such locutions, it has only to abandon itself; it is useless to desire or not to desire them, for there is nothing to repulse, nothing to fear. The soul ought not even to seek to effect what is said, for God never utters substantial words in order that we should translate them into acts; He Himself brings about their effect. This is what distinguishes them from successive and formal locutions.... Illusion is not to be feared here, for neither the understanding nor the devil can interfere in this matter.... Substantial words are therefore a powerful means of union with God.... Happy the souls to which God addresses them.[57]

A good example of a locution is found in the autobiography of St. Teresa of Jesus:

---

[56] Aumann, *Spiritual Theology*, 427.
[57] St. John of the Cross, *The Ascent of Mount Carmel*, bk. 2, chap. 31.

Once, when I was very restless and upset, unable to recollect myself, battling and striving, turning all the time in thought to things that were not perfect, and imagining I was not detached as I used to be, I was afraid, seeing how wicked I was, that the favors which the Lord had granted me might be illusions. In short, my soul was in great darkness. While I was distressed in this way, the Lord began to speak to me and told me not to be troubled; the state in which I found myself would show me how miserable I should be if He withdrew from me; while we lived in this flesh we were never safe.[58]

And later she wrote: "Then He said to me: 'Ah, daughter, how few are they who love Me in truth! If people loved Me, I should not hide my secrets from them.'"[59]

In the life of St. Josemaría Escrivá there are also instances of locutions. Andres Vazquez de Prada gave the following account in his biography of the founder of Opus Dei. One event took place on August 7, 1931 and is described in a letter written in 1947. "I am embarrassed about this," he confesses before beginning the story, "but I am writing it to you in response to indications I have received. I will not however, tell you many of these things." He then continues:

That day of the Transfiguration, while celebrating Holy Mass at the Foundation for the Sick (on a side altar), when I raised the host, there was another voice without the sound of speech. A voice perfectly clear as always, said, *Et ego, si exaltatus fuero a terra, omnia traham ad me*

---

[58] *The Life of St. Teresa of Jesus*, 346.
[59] Ibid., 388.

ipsum! [And I, when I am lifted up from the earth, will draw all things to myself! (John 12:32)]. And here is what I mean by this: I am not saying it in the sense in which it is said in Scripture. I say it to you meaning that you should put me at the pinnacle of all human activities, so that in every place in the world there will be Christians with a dedication that is personal and totally free—Christians who will be other Christs.[60]

A little later, the author continues: "Around the year 1930, [Our Lord] made this locution clearly heard, not just once but a number of times: *"Et fui tecum in omnibus ubicumque ambulasti"* [2 Sam. 7:9]—I have been and will be with you wherever you go."[61]

In 1958, in London, St. Josemaría had the following experience, which he recounted to his sons in a meditation in Rome:

A little over a month ago, I was in a country that I love a lot. It's full of sects and heresies, and there's a pervasive indifference to the things of God. Contemplating this panorama, I grew distressed, I felt incompetent, helpless: "Josemaría, here you can't do anything," I was right. By myself I couldn't accomplish a single thing; without God, I couldn't even manage to pick up a straw from the ground. It was so obvious that I was totally ineffective that I almost became sad. And that is bad. How can a son of God become sad? He can get tired, because he is pulling the cart like a faithful donkey. But sad, no. Sadness is a bad thing!

60 Andres Vazquez de Prada, *The Founder of Opus Dei*, vol.1 (New York: Scepter, 2001), 287.
61 Ibid., 291.

Suddenly, in the middle of the street where people from every part of the world were coming and going, I felt within me, in the depths of my heart, the efficacy of God's strength: "You, no; you can't do anything. But I—I can do everything. You are ineptitude, but I am omnipotence. I will be with you and make you effective! We will draw souls to happiness, to unity, to the path of the Lord, to salvation! Here, too, we will sow abundant peace and joy!"[62]

Locutions are sparks of light benefiting chosen ones, and from them they radiate to those who welcome these flashes of light.

The Divine Call

One of the outstanding supernatural phenomena that occur with relative frequency is what we commonly know as a "vocation." God calls a person to follow Him and give his life to Him. The person who has heard the whisper of God has experienced the veil becoming less impenetrable.

A vocation is a supernatural grace that has no adequate human explanation and is always somewhat mysterious. It brings about inner changes in the recipient: the person starts going to daily Mass, stops going to parties, breaks off with his fiancée or her boyfriend, studies more intensely, prays more. The explanation is in the gift the person has received from God, who has enabled him to discover realities heretofore veiled. Understood this way, there is no doubt that every vocation is a disclosure of the concealed God to a person who freely receives the gift of the call.

[62] Ibid., 238.

Why God Hides

The book of Isaiah gives a splendid example of a divine call:

In the year that King Uzziah died I saw the Lord sitting upon a throne, high and lifted up; and his train filled the temple. Above him stood the seraphim; each had six wings: with two he covered his face, and with two he covered his feet, and with two he flew. And one called to another and said: "Holy, holy, holy is the LORD of hosts; the whole earth is full of his glory." ...

Then flew one of the seraphim to me, having in his hand a burning coal which he had taken with tongs from the altar. And he touched my mouth, and said: "Behold, this has touched your lips; your guilt is taken away, and your sin forgiven." And I heard the voice of the Lord saying, "Whom shall I send, and who will go for us?" Then I said, "Here am I! Send me" (6:1–3, 6–8).

Alfonso Aguiló, a noted Spanish author, devoted a chapter of his book *La Llamada de Dios* to the way God acts when He calls people to His service. In the chapter "Dios habla bajito" (God speaks in a low voice), he notes that many people consider being more generous with God and with others but do not take the final step. They are restless but do not know if that is due to their vocation. Aguiló explains that in most cases, God speaks with a quiet voice, like the whisper of a gentle breeze. Vocation is an encounter that gives an inspiration to life, from which is born a commitment to the plan God has for someone. The vocation includes all that a person sees himself called to do, what gives meaning to his life.[63] Aguiló adds:

---

[63] Alfonso Aguiló, *La Llamada de Dios* (Madrid: Ediciones Palabra, 2009), 69–76.

The lives of the saints show that God usually makes His will known in a simple manner, through ordinary things — within the family, through a friend, a book, a sickness, and other normal things.

If God were to make His will known by means of bursts of light, apparitions, angelic shouts or similar things, our freedom would be very much diminished under the power of the divine light. God prefers the clear darkness of the faith, which is reached though prayer. When He calls us, He hides a bit, perhaps because He wants to leave some room for our freedom. Otherwise, it would not be a love story anymore.[64]

A genuine supernatural vocation is always a manifestation of the hidden God. And yet in most cases, He prefers to remain withdrawn in deference to our freedom, the key to merit and to recompense.

Piercing the Veil in Ordinary Life

With the help of God providing the gift of faith, the separating veil can also become thinner in ordinary life. It is when we manage to discover "that something divine" hidden in the most prosaic and earthly realities of day-to-day life.

Thus, with a supernatural outlook, certain coincidences will not appear as mere fortuitous events, but as providential arrangements. It is the hidden God playing the game of daily life with His children. More importantly, everyday life, with its family, work, social, and recreational dimensions, can provide opportunities to encounter the Lord.

[64] Ibid., 71.

Why God Hides

At the canonization of St. Josemaría Escrivá, Pope John Paul II described him as "the saint of the ordinary life." It was a fitting characterization, for St. Josemaría always emphasized the need to find the Supreme Being in and through the ordinary circumstances of life. To do so amounts to piercing the veil that covers the "other, supernatural world." In a homily he delivered at a Holy Mass on the campus of the University of Navarra on October 8, 1967, he stated:

> Your daily encounter with Christ takes place where your fellow men, your yearnings, your work, and your affections are. It is in the midst of the most material things of the earth that we must sanctify ourselves, serving God and all mankind.
>
> This I have been teaching all the time, using words of the Holy Scripture: the world is not evil, because it comes from the hands of God, because it is His creation, because Yahweh looked upon it and saw that it was good. It is we ourselves, men and women, who make it evil and ugly with our sins and unfaithfulness. Don't doubt it, my children: any attempt to escape from the noble reality of daily life, for you men and women of the world, is something opposed to the will of God.
>
> On the contrary, you must realize now, more clearly than ever, that God is calling you to serve Him in and from the ordinary, secular and civil activities of human life. He waits for us every day, in the laboratory, in the operating theater, in the army barracks, in the university chair, in the factory, in the workshop, in the fields, in the home, and in all the immense panorama of work. Understand this well: there is something holy, something

divine in the most ordinary situations, and it is up to each one of you to discover it. . . .

There is no other way, my daughters and sons: either we learn to find our Lord in ordinary, everyday life, or we shall never find Him. That is why I tell you that our age needs to give back to matter and to the apparently trivial events of life their noble, original meaning. It needs to place them at the service of the Kingdom of God; it needs to spiritualize them, turning them into a means and an occasion for a continual meeting with Jesus Christ. . . .

This doctrine of Sacred Scripture, as you know, is to be found in the very core of the spirit of Opus Dei. It should lead you to do your work perfectly, to love God and your fellowmen by putting love in the little things of everyday life and discovering that divine something which is hidden in small details. These lines of a Castilian poet are especially appropriate here: "Write slowly and with a careful hand, for doing things well is more important than doing them." . . .

Let me consider another aspect of everyday life which is particularly dear to me. I refer to human love, to the noble love between a man and a woman, to courtship and to marriage. . . .

Love that leads to marriage and family can also be a marvelous divine way, a vocation, a path for a complete dedication to our God. Do things perfectly, I have reminded you. Put love into the little duties of each day; discover that divine something contained in these details. All this teaching has a special place in that area of life where human love has its setting. . . .

Besides, you cannot fail to realize that only among those who understand and value in all its depth what we have just considered about human love, can there arise another ineffable insight of which Jesus speaks: an insight which is pure gift of God, moving a person to surrender body and soul to the Lord, to offer Him an undivided heart, without the mediation of earthly love....

Let us live by faith. Let us take up the shield of faith, the helmet of salvation and the sword of the Spirit, which is God's Word.

It is by faith, therefore, that the dividing veil is opened up a bit, and the real and true meaning of ordinary things and events comes out.

4

The Human Condition

[The Lord] dwells in inapproachable light,
whom no man has ever seen.

—1 Timothy 6:16

From all eternity, God has called man to *see*: to see Him by faith in this life on earth, and to see Him by vision in the life to come. Man's destiny is therefore one of vision. "There," all is light; "here," there is a mixture of light and dark, and man walks in shadows. To fail to "look up," to fail to see things with a supernatural outlook, is to grope in the dark.

Baptismal grace removes the obstacle posed by original sin. The other increases in sanctifying grace, which come chiefly from the worthy reception of the other sacraments, facilitate the vision of faith in this life and the vision of glory in eternity. It is a process that consists in a journey from the light of faith (*lumen fidei*) to the light of glory (*lumen gloriae*).

The supreme tragedy for man is to fail in the great test of life and to be deprived forever of the vision of the manifest God.

The horror of this failure is expressed in Psalm 87:

I am reckoned among those who go down to the Pit;
    I am a man who has no strength,
like one forsaken among the dead,
    like the slain that lie in the grave,
like those whom thou dost remember no more,
    for they are cut off from thy hand (vv. 4–5)

Since man has a strong tendency to focus on himself, he needs to strive to put himself aside in order to see and adore the hidden Lover and to pay attention to Him. If man does not adore the Almighty, he will end up adoring himself.

What Is Man Doing Here on Earth?

We are a redeemed people, living in exile, called to serve and love the unseen Savior through faith, hope, and love.[65] This is done with the help of the Church, which continues Christ's work on earth. Man's present situation resembles being in front of a one-way mirror, for God sees us perfectly, but we do not see Him.

In his Second Letter to the Corinthians, St. Paul gives an exposition of the human condition:

So we are always of good courage; we know that while we are at home in the body, we are away from the Lord, for we walk by faith, not by sight. We are of good courage, and we would rather be away from the body and at home with the Lord. So whether we are at home or away, we make it our aim to please Him. For we must all appear

---

[65] Redeemed by Jesus Christ, we need His merits to be applied subjectively to each one of us. In this sense, we are sinners in need of redemption.

before the judgment seat of Christ, so that each one may receive good or evil, according to what he has done in the body (5:6–10).

Cardinal Ratzinger described the same situation as follows:

Of course, one can still ask why God did not make a world in which His presence is more evident, why Christ did not leave the world with another sign of His presence so radiant that no one could resist it. This is the mystery of God and man, which we find in this world where God is not so manifest as tangible things are, but can be sought and found only when the heart sets out on the "exodus from Egypt."[66]

In this text, Benedict XVI expresses the universal aspiration of all mankind to see the Lord—which constitutes the premise of these pages. He points the way to reach this goal: set out on an "exodus from Egypt." The pope alludes to the Israelites' attachment to the material advantages in Egypt, as they journeyed toward the Promised Land. The scenario is an excellent parallel to man's present situation, in which he must leave behind his earthly attachments as he journeys toward his promised land.

Cardinal Julian Herranz's description of man's situation is poetic:

How much I want to understand You, and I do not understand You; how much I want to believe in You, and I do not believe in You.

How much I want to find You, and I do not find You.

---

[66] Benedict XVI, *Jesus of Nazareth*, 34.

How much I want to have You, and I do not have You;
how much I want to love You, and I do not love You.

You are there, waiting for me, further than the winter.
And You are here in the things of the earth and of time
where the eternal walking has already begun.

The "eternal walking" has already begun for us as we march
forward on this earth of ours.

Materialism versus Faith

The present situation could also be described in this way: The
Maker is totally inaccessible and covered as if by a veil, out of
sight of the eyes of flesh and other sensory powers. At the same
time, a multitude of invitations to indulge in material goods bom-
bard the senses. Overindulgence in some of these goods could
be contrary to His will, and a choice must be made between the
goods and His will. In these moments, testing is taking place. The
decision marks the distinction between the materialistic person,
who has lost much of the Maker's presence, and the believer,
who pierces the veil with his supernatural vision and chooses
to do His will. The decision of the moment will depend on how
important God is to a person, how clear He is in the person's
mind, and on how much the person believes in and loves Him.

A Stratified View

The classic definition of prayer is the raising of one's mind and
heart to God.[67] The verb "raising" connotes a stratified view. St.

---

[67] St. John Damascene, *De Fide Orthodoxa*, 3:24.

Paul exhorts us, "Set your minds on things that are above" (Col. 3:2). It is an invitation to locate Christ's kingdom "up there," above the earth, in the concept of stratification.

The greatest call to this way of viewing things is in Christ's Ascension, which drew the hearts and the eyes of the disciples upward. He chose to depart from this earth in a very dramatic manner. That day, a sizeable number of His disciples saw Him going up to Heaven. The Acts of the Apostles gives this description:

> And when he had said this, as they were looking on, he was lifted up, and a cloud took him out of their sight. And while they were gazing into heaven as he went, behold, two men stood by them in white robes, and said, "Men of Galilee, why do you stand looking into heaven? This Jesus, who was taken up from you into heaven, will come in the same way as you saw him go into heaven" (1:9–11).

"A cloud took him out of their sight." On the day of His Ascension, Christ went to the right side of the Father. He will no longer be visible until His Second Coming. He will be covered by a cloud—that is to say, he will be a veiled Lover, and that cloud will have to be pierced by the rays of faith.

"In this our exile," we perceive only our fellow men; those in the upper and nether worlds remain invisible. In the upper world are all the "cloud of heavenly witnesses" (Heb. 11:1)—the angels and the saints, whose identification with the will of the Maker found expression in their eternal cry: I will serve! In the netherworld, the realm of Satan, the Anti-Christ, and the damned, the cry is an eternal "I will not serve!" Satan and the souls of the damned are forever opposed to Jesus Christ, the Logos. People on earth are prevented from viewing both worlds. The faithful benefit from heavenly influences while enduring diabolical temptations, walking in the light of reason and faith while groping in shadows and ever longing for the eternal vision.

Now, our task is to pierce the veil that covers the silent and secluded King by means of faith, hope, and love, and in so doing to fulfill His first commandment: "You shall love the Lord your God with all your heart, and with all your soul, and with all your mind" (Matt. 22:37–38).

What Our Lives Are

In a parable, Christ describes what life on earth is like: "A nobleman went into a far country to receive kingly power and then return. Calling ten of his servants, he gave them ten pounds and said to them: trade with them till I come" (Luke 19:12–12). This is the way Jesus envisions our lives: He is the nobleman who goes to a distant country. The distance is so great that, without His help, no one can cover the expanse. He is shielded, silent, and distant, and yet He is closer to us than we are to ourselves. These two characteristics of Jesus Christ appear contradictory, but they are compatible. He will come back at the moment of our death (for each of us individually) and at the Second Coming.

The parallel between the parable and the reality of Christian life is also found in the attitude of the nobleman. He has gone away but has not lost interest in what his servants are doing. So it is with the Lord. He has gone into hiding, and as in the parable, there will be reckoning and retribution in the end.

Benedict XVI, in his first encyclical, *Deus Caritas Est*, quotes a passage from the first letter of St. John: "We have known and believe the love that God has for us," and he calls it the "synthetic formulation of Christian existence."[68] He sees the search and the ensuing discovery of the unseen Lover as the main task of every Christian—nay, of every human being. For we are, without exception, called to look for Him, to find Him, and to love Him and to help others to do the same.

This is our task: to pierce the veil and enter the cloud while passing through the only way and the only door that exists: Jesus Christ, our Savior.

Our Lord pointed to the importance of faith in our task. When He was asked: "What must we do, to be doing the works of God?" Jesus replied, "This is the work of God, that you believe in him whom he has sent" (John 6:28).

In saying, "No one can come to me unless the Father who sent me draws him" (John 6:44), Christ teaches us that piercing the veil is not something that we do on our own, but always in cooperation with Him. It is as if the invisible Father were throwing ropes to us who have fallen into a dark pit and need help to come out to the light. We have to grab the rope.

We still have to seek Him as we walk in shadows, illumined by His mysterious light. "We walk by faith," says St. Paul (2 Cor. 5:7), and Elizabeth exclaimed to Mary: "Blessed is she who believed" (Luke 1:45). By her faith, Mary pierced the veil that covers the transcendent world. This is at the root of Mary's greatness and happiness.

---

[68] Benedict XVI, Encyclical *Deus Caritas Est* (December 25, 2005), no. 1.

5

Man's Deep Longing

---

*As a hart longs for flowing streams, so longs my soul
for thee, O God. My soul thirsts for God, for the living
God. When shall I come and behold the face of God?*

—Psalm 42:1–2

There is a "vital anguish," as Heidegger calls it, for God in this
earth, where humans bear the weight of deprivation, loneliness,
and longing for the One most needed. The great Étienne Gilson
says, "By intelligence the soul is capable of Truth; by love it is
capable of the Good; its torment arises from the fact that it seeks
it without knowing what it is that it seeks and, consequently,
without knowing where to look for it."[69]

There is a universal eagerness to remove the obstacle, the
veil that covers the supernatural world from natural perception.
To see God ought to be the highest aspiration of all human
beings. This is why the saints, men and women of God, make
their own the words of the psalmist: "Thy face, LORD, do I seek.

---

[69] Étienne Gilson, *The Spirit of Mediaeval Philosophy* (Indiana:
University of Notre Dame Press, 1991), 173.

Hide not thy face from me" (Ps. 27:8–9). God is the goal of the inquisitive mind, the will that is eager to love without limits, and the restless heart.

A Natural Longing

The psalmist tells us: "One thing I ask the LORD, and I seek after: to live in the house of the LORD all the days of my life, to behold the beauty of the LORD, and to inquire in his temple" (Ps. 27:4). Very conscious of the fact that man was created to see the First Principle, St. Augustine wrote: "Lord, I have been created to contemplate You, and I have not achieved that for which I was created!"[70] "A longing for God," as Karl Adam beautifully expressed, "is the natural dowry of the human soul, its immortal jewelry, the most illuminating of the sparks of the divine love which are shed on human nature."[71] St. Josemaría attests that "the desire for God comes from the deepest recesses of the heart of man."[72]

The thirst for God is common to all because we were made by God and for Him. The restlessness of the heart, the desire for eternal happiness, for fulfillment, to love and to be loved, is nothing but the thirst for the veiled God. It is a thirst that only He can satisfy.

Writing to the Corinthians, St. Paul expresses the nostalgic desire for the vision of the Lord:

For we know that if the earthly tent we live in is destroyed, we have a building from God, a house not made with hands,

---

[70] St. Augustine, *Proslogion*, chap. 1.

[71] Adam, *The Son of God*.

[72] Josemaría Escrivá, *Christ Is Passing By*, no. 175.

eternal in the heavens. Here indeed we groan, and long to put on our heavenly dwelling, so that by putting it on we may not be found naked. For while we are still in this tent, we sigh with anxiety (2 Cor. 5:1–4).

St. Thomas Aquinas ended his celebrated hymn "*Adoro Te Devote*" with these lines: "Jesus, for the present seen as through a mask, give me what I thirst for, give me what I ask: let me see your glory in a blaze of light. And instead of blindness give me, Lord, my sight."[73]

Touched by that sentence in the Gospel of St. John, "Sir, we wish to see Jesus" (12:21), José María Muntadas shows how this "longing to see God"[74] was found in the hearts of the shepherds who went to the stable of Bethlehem, among the Magi who were guided by a star, and in Zacchaeus, the tax collector of short stature who climbed a sycamore tree to get a view of Jesus. Muntadas talks about the innate nostalgia for the vision of God by explaining that this longing is not cold or intellectual but involves the heart. As a result of our elevation to the supernatural order as children of God, obtained for us by Christ, that radical nostalgia has become a vehement desire of a son to see his Father. Thanks to the gift of wisdom, the soul comes to look at everything in the bright light of the Triune God and judges things with divine sense.

Muntadas explains:

[This longing] generates in us dealings with the Divine Persons, thus participating in the Trinitarian Life. Then, even though external occupations fill our day, or sufferings

---

[73] *Iesu, quem velatum nunc aspicio, oro fiat quot tam sitio; ut te revelata cernens facie, visu sim beatus tuae gloriae.*

[74] José María Muntadas, *El Anhelo de Dios* (Madrid: Folletos Mundo Cristiano, 1993), 11.

weigh heavily on our heart, we feel in our soul the divine presence, and we never abandon the desire of His company. Thus, the Christian virtue of Hope takes the human longing for God and elevates it to the supernatural level. It tells us that this desire for God that the soul experiences now is authentic; that it carries a seed of great promises made by God, and that the manifestation of its fullness will be greater than what we could imagine.[75]

Muntadas adds:

The years will pass, the body will fall apart due to daily work, and the heart will fall in love more and more with God.... At the pace of love the divine longing will grow until all else becomes small; there is prayer without words; the tabernacle, bigger; the joys more magnificent; the sorrows more appreciated; in the lips one single word; and in the heart only God.[76]

"Hunger for God," wrote Bishop Alvaro del Portillo, "cannot be satisfied in this world, and so we seek complete union in eternity."[77]

Much earlier, the tower of Babel had been a futile attempt to reach the heavens and to see God: "Come, let us build ourselves a city, and a tower with its top in the heavens" (Gen. 11:4). It was one more expression (albeit mistaken) of that general longing.

In spite of all that Yahweh had done for them, the Israelites in the desert, tired of worshipping an invisible God, built

[75] Ibid.

[76] Ibid., 38.

[77] Alvaro del Portillo, foreword to Josemaría Escrivá, *The Forge* (Manila: Sinag-tala Publishers, 2000), 560.

themselves a golden calf that they could see and touch. They abandoned the concealed Lord for a visible idol.

Throughout their journey, the Jews kept a keen longing for the land of Canaan. Now, in a similar way, we too experience a longing for our Fatherland.

This common anguish on earth is reflected in the antiphon of Lauds of the Saturday of the First Week in Ordinary Time, which asks the Lord to illumine those who sit in darkness and under the shadow of death. It expresses the feeling experienced in this world while awaiting the light of His vision in the life hereafter. This longing in the midst of shadows, as experienced by countless persons, including great saints such as St. Teresa of Jesus and St. John of the Cross, has been called the dark night of the soul. St. John of the Cross wrote in the first stanza of his *Spiritual Canticle*: "Where have you hidden, beloved, and left me with my grieving?"

Alfonso Aguiló recounts how, in 1956, Mother Teresa of Calcutta told the archbishop of that city, "I want to be an apostle of joy." But by a mysterious disposition of Divine Providence, she sometimes carried her apostolate of cheerfulness in the midst of an unbearable dryness: "Occasionally," she said, "the agony of God's absence is so great, and alongside it the vivid desire for the Absent is so profound, that the only prayer that I am still able to recite is 'Sacred Heart of Jesus, I trust in you. I will satiate your thirst for souls.'"[78]

The Thirst for God

St. Teresa said: "O my delight, Lord of all created things and my God! How long must I wait to see You? What remedy do You

[78] Alfonso Aguiló, *La Llamada de Dios*, 284.

provide for one who finds so little on earth that might give some rest apart from You?"[79]

Together with the longing for the life to come, St. Josemaría had very much in mind our remaining tasks on this earth. In a meditation he gave in 1972, he said:

> Every instant of our lives has an eternal meaning. My children, this world is passing; it is not in our hands. We cannot waste time, which is short. We must really set ourselves to the task of personal sanctification and of our apostolic work. The Lord has entrusted it to us; we must *spend* it faithfully, loyally, and administer it well. We must use the talents we have received with a sense of responsibility.[80]

During our earthly exile, we experience both the need for the Almighty and the deprivation of the vision of Him. This makes for suffering. Endowed only with the poor and partial vision of things, we have a nostalgia for the lost Paradise and a deep, intuitive longing for Heaven, where the total vision is to be found. Man was made for that; his entire being pines for that! He was created for Heaven. Hence, in this earthly exile, his deepest vital anguish, his most insatiable thirst can be satisfied only by the discovery, the loving encounter with the now secluded Lover. The psalmist says it clearly: "The LORD is my light and my salvation" (Ps. 27:1).

"Hide not thy face from me,"-exclaimed King David (Ps. 143:7), and Psalm 89 echoes this anguish: "How long, O Lord? Will thou hide thyself forever?" (v. 46).

---

[79] St. Teresa of Avila, *The Autobiography, Soliloquies* (New York: Book-of-the-Month Club, 1995), 448.

[80] St. Josemaría Escrivá, "Time for Reparation," February 1972.

The longing for the Lover grows hand in hand with contemplation. Now we see Him under obscure images, for "it does not yet appear what we shall be, but we know that when he appears we shall be like him, for we shall see him as he is" (1 John 3:2).

That deep desire for God, found in our hearts and experienced in varying degrees, can be articulated by the expression "*Maranatha!* Come, Lord, Jesus!" (Rev. 22:20) and by those words that our Lord Himself taught us: "Thy kingdom come!"

With God's help, man manages to remove, as it were, bit by bit, the veil covering the shielded Lover. In so doing, he experiences great joy and consolation. This is not surprising, for the Creator made man for the light, not for darkness. They make their own this saying of St. Paul: "For He is our peace, He has made us both one, and has broken down the dividing wall of hostility" (Eph. 2:14).

Lukewarm persons feel annoyed by the present situation. In their inability to see the Lord and the other persons of the supernatural world, they seek an excuse for their lack of faith. They ask: "Where is God? Where can He be found? Is He hiding somewhere?" They argue that they could be vibrant and dedicated to the Ultimate Being, were He not so remote and concealed.

Agnostics point to that veil as the reason for their attitude, saying, "We do not know, and nobody can know anything about God, whether He really exists; let us therefore ignore Him."

Atheists defy the veil. They say they would believe only if there were evident, sensible, and verifiable proofs of His existence and action in the world.

The cause of the deepest longing that man has — this *vital anguish* — is the need for God. This need is coupled with the fact that He is outside of man's sense perception. Since He is a Spirit without any matter, He cannot be seen.

Why God Hides

But the Almighty looks at man with infinite care and love. As the inspired psalmist sang: "The LORD looks down from heaven, he sees all the sons of men; from where he sits enthroned he looks forth on all the inhabitants of the earth, he who fashions the hearts of them all, and observes all their deeds" (Ps. 33:13–15).

Different Ways of Longing for God's Vision

There are different manners of wanting to see God. One is the way of the person who is tired of living "in expectation." He wants evidence to satisfy his mind, which tells him that there must be Someone behind everything — in the wonders of nature, for example. He does not want to trust, for to believe in God always implies trusting Him. He is curious about the identity of that Someone but is uncomfortable about not being able to perceive Him with his senses. He blames the Maker for not manifesting Himself. The situation could be compared to the case of one who smells something burning and goes out anxiously to find what is causing it. Annoyed because he does not see the flames, he says, "There is no fire!"

A different way of longing for the Lover's face is found in the individual who believes in God. He is eager to see Him because he is in love with the secluded Lover and is eager to see Him, as all love-struck persons are. This is the case, for instance, of St. Teresa of Jesus, who, toward the end of her life, kept repeating: "Jesus, it is about time that we see each other!"[81]

In both cases there is desire, even impatience, to see the Lord, but only in the second instance is the motive a good one, for it is prompted by faith, hope, and love.

[81] *Jesus, ya va siendo hora de que nos veamos!*

To Cross the Barrier

The desire to know the future with certitude is universal. It includes eagerness to unveil the mystery of life. It shows itself in a longing to penetrate the divide that separates not only today from tomorrow but also this temporal world from the next, the human from the divine. Superstitious beliefs such as the horoscope are related to this desire.

In the last moments of a dying person, when someone—a doctor or a nurse—says, "He or she is gone!" it is likely that a question comes to mind: "Gone? But, where?" In those moments, the reality of the gulf, the partition that separates this world from the next, is keenly felt; and death appears as a jump from this world to the other world behind the partition.

If the desire to see the concealed Father is universal, scholars devoted to the study of the things of God—theologians—could be expected to experience this yearning in a special manner. Along these lines, Benedict XVI said: "For me, theology is the attempt to get to know the Beloved better."[82] In the pope's mind, theologians are to undertake not just a cold, scientific research concerning the Supreme Being but a loving search for the shielded Lover.

"Ya Va Siendo Hora Que Nos Veamos!"

Jose Luis Olayzola beautifully described the death of a beloved saint:

As St. Teresa of Jesus was laid on her deathbed, she sensed the presence of the Beloved. Her face was

---

[82] Peter Seewald, *Benedict XVI* (San Francisco: Ignatius Press, 2005), 62.

transfigured, and with a youthful air she exclaimed, "The time has come for us to behold one another, my Beloved and my Lord. The hour has come for me to quit this barren place and for my soul to revel in You, as I have so yearned to do.[83]

The saint of Avila had dealt with the Divine Lover for many years through the veil that separated her from Him. She had eagerly waited for the moment in which the veil would be removed and the view would no longer be obstructed.

From the earliest times human beings have looked at Heaven as their lost Paradise. The hearts were made for happiness, but they remained deprived of vision and fulfillment as a consequence of sin. St. Augustine pointed to our anguished situation when he wrote, "We are created for You, Lord, and our hearts are restless until they rest in You."[84]

In Shadows Only

In dealings with persons of the supernatural world, there are two main characteristics. One is the discomfort due to not being able to see face-to-face the person one is talking to. The second comes in handy: the certainty that the interlocutor is truly there, a certainty based on faith.

These two combined give rise to a semi-light, a *chiaroscuro*, a state of affairs that may be called "seeing in the midst of shadows." It is the vision characteristic of the journey on earth that, while illumined by faith and reason, strikes a sharp contrast with both

---

[83] Jose Luis Olayzola, *The Loves of Teresa of Avila* (Manila: Sinagtala, 1999), 169.

[84] St. Augustine, *Confessions*, bk. 1, chap. 1.

the perfect light of Heaven and the total darkness of Hell. This uncomfortable condition creates a yearning for the Beatific Vision in the Eternal Day, as well as a dread of the perpetual Night of Hell.

Become One More Witness from Above

The Christian's hope is that after death, in the life hereafter, he will join the "joyful family of unseen witnesses," to become "one more veiled spectator" of the human drama, in which, with faith, hope, and love, his fellow Christians are called to make responsible use of their power of self-determination. This means their entire lives have to be centered on the Lord, the object of their deepest longing, the source of all spiritual strength. They are to seek Him, adore Him, long to be united with Him and help others to do the same. They are able to obtain much of that union with the God-Man in the Eucharist, in that lovely and sacred mystery where there is a divine pledge of complete union that is expected to be attained fully in the life to come.

Not a Lonely Search

The search for the Living Lord is a very personal endeavor. It is a task assigned to each person individually and in a nontransferable way. Each one has to engage in this search. And yet, thanks to the sterling Communion of Saints, it is an accompanied affair. The Triune God is the most interested; He is the one who decreed this present exile that will determine man's future status in eternal life. The Lord always helps in the search and in the finding.

God the Father has the interest of an infinitely loving Father for the well-being of His children. God the Son has the interest of a Redeemer who wants to see the fruits of His costly Redemption. God the Holy Spirit is witnessing man's free response to His unceasing work of sanctification.

The Blessed Mother, Mary, follows the pilgrim steps of her children too, as no other mother would do on earth. Joseph does the same as the Virgin does, as do the angels and the souls in Purgatory, to the extent that God gives them power to do so.

The entire Church on earth also provides continuous assistance, sending (as St. Josemaría was fond of saying) *arterial blood*, which provides oxygen to the cells. This is done mostly in the form of anonymous prayers and sacrifices coming from countless fellowmen.

There is also the guidance of the legitimate shepherds, the pope, the bishops, and priests, as well as the edifying and warm encouragement provided by brothers and sisters in the Faith, most especially relatives and friends.

Therefore, it is not a lonely search. Because he communes with God's family in the company of witnesses, the Christian's call has a wonderful ecclesial and social dimension.

6

God's Ways

Then he also went up, not publicly, but as it were in private.

—John 7:10

As man relates with the veiled Lord, he observes certain patterns in His ways with us that could help us in grasping His loving designs. Without pretending to comprehend all His plans, which are divine and mysterious, we can detect recurring features in His ways that fit His image of a loving and merciful Father.

Pebbles Thrown by the Shepherd

A priest friend of mine said to me once, "I am very thankful to the veiled Shepherd, for He is helping me a lot in my struggle against pride. Often, when I indulge in some thoughts of self-complacency, He humiliates me by allowing me to make a mistake in some way right then and there. For instance, on one occasion, I was celebrating the Holy Mass and the thought came to my mind that I was able to recite very well and by heart the words of the Canon. A few seconds after this, the one serving called my attention to an oversight on my part. To me it was a clear warning, like a little pebble thrown at me by the Good and Silent Shepherd, who wanted to teach me a lesson and did not want me to go astray."

I thought that this was a good example of the ways our hidden Teacher and Shepherd keeps us on the right track. They are displays of love and of wisdom, for He gently corrects and helps us while remaining in the background to keep us free.

Only to an Extent and for a Period

The Almighty acts extraordinarily only when necessary and only for as long as needed. In the Acts of the Apostles is an account of how an angel freed Peter from prison. When the two of them had passed the first and the second guards, they came to an iron gate, which opened of its own accord. They went on to the street leading to the city, and the angel left Peter, who came to himself and said, "Now I am sure that the Lord has sent his angel and rescued me from all that the Jewish people were expecting" (Acts 12:11). This is the usual modus operandi of the Almighty: He discloses Himself on occasion for a minimum amount of time, and the rest is left to the exercise of human initiative and freedom.

St. Matthew narrates two other cases. The Magi from the east were "warned in a dream not to return to Herod, so they departed for their own country by another way" (2:12). It was a supernatural warning that did not include the extraordinary action of God's providence for the rest of the trip. The other case concerns Joseph, the spouse of Mary: "An angel of the Lord appeared to Joseph in a dream and said, 'Rise, take the child and his mother, and flee to Egypt, and remain there till I tell you; for Herod is about to search for the child, to destroy him.' And he rose and took the child and his mother by night and departed to Egypt" (2:13–14).

God's Suddenness

The book of Wisdom tells us that "the righteous man will stand with great confidence in the presence of those who have afflicted him, and those who made light of his labors. When they see him, they will be shaken with dreadful fear, and they will be amazed at his unexpected salvation" (Wisd. 5:1–2). Suddenness in revealing Himself is another characteristic of the ways of the veiled God. He exhibits this trait in collective as well as in individual revelations. A supernatural revelation is always a break from the usual sequence of events, for they are unexpected, and so take protagonists by surprise. To manifest Himself or His agency in a sudden manner is something that fits well with His condition as a hiding Lover. This is how Saul of Tarsus met Christ: "Now as he journeyed he approached Damascus, and suddenly a light from heaven flashed about him" (Acts 9:3).

Not only the Maker's appearances but also those of other heavenly personages, such as Our Lady and some saints, are characterized by suddenness. This was the case both in Lourdes and in Fatima. St. Bernadette Soubirous wrote of her experience in this account:

> After the others had picked up some pieces of wood under the grotto, they disappeared along the Gave River. When I was alone I threw stones into the bed of the river to get a foothold, but it was of no use. So I had to make up my mind to take off my sabots and cross the canal as Jeanne and my sister had done.

Why God Hides

I had just begun to take off my first stocking when suddenly I heard a great noise like the sound of a storm. Almost at the same time there came out of the interior of the grotto a golden-colored cloud. Soon after, a Lady — young and beautiful, exceedingly beautiful, the likes of whom I had never seen — came and placed herself at the entrance of the opening above the rosebush.[85]

Of Fatima, Fr. John J. Delaney wrote this account:

On May 13, 1917, in almost the same spot where, the year before, the Angel had appeared to them, the children were once more tending their sheep in the Chousa Velha in the section known as the Cova da Iria. They had said the Rosary, finished their meager lunch, and begun to play when suddenly, out of an azure sky, a brilliant flash of light appeared.

God's action in souls is often similarly marked by suddenness. A friend of mine wrote in a note:

Thank you, my God, for the times, few but memorable, in which, in spite of my unworthiness, You have touched my soul. Those touches have always been a jubilant surprise, a sudden irruption, a passing experience. How I wish that they had lasted forever. They have always left me with deep peace and an indescribable joy. They have been a great, serene, and intimate impulse, a confirmation, and a big help. In those moments, you were not for me a concealed God. Thank you, Lord! I did not deserve them!

[85] John J. Delaney, *A Woman Clothed with the Sun* (Manila: Sinagtala, 1988), 122.

How clear it appears that those graces were all the work of Your mercy. So, I will sing forever Your mercies![86]

God's disappearance also often occurs suddenly, as in when Jesus manifested Himself to the two disciples on the way to Emmaus: "When He was at table with them, He took the bread and blessed, and broke it, and gave it to them. And their eyes were opened and they recognized Him." St. Luke adds immediately, "And He vanished out of their sight" (Luke 24:30–31).

God's Gentleness

In the matter of the apostolate, the silent Lord does not grant fruits without man's effort. Since these fruits are miracles of grace, the Almighty wants our prayers, atonement, and action, *so that His divine hand is covered.* As always, He wishes to act discreetly in respect for man's freedom.

The Church describes God's rule as *most gentle* (*suavissimo imperio*), a characteristic of the way the Supreme Being acts. This gentle rule is made possible by His being withdrawn. Were He visible and patent, His rule would be overpowering. Were He to manifest Himself to us in His majestic power, we would be terrified. But the Lord does not want terrified servants or slaves, only confident and loving children. This is one reason He shields Himself.

St. Josemaría explained the quiet way the Lord acts within us in the following passage:

The action of the Holy Spirit can pass unnoticed, because God does not reveal to us his plans, and because man's

---

[86] *Misericordias tuas in aeternum cantabo!*

sin clouds over the divine gifts. But faith reminds us that God is always acting. He has created us and maintains us in existence, and he leads all creation by his grace towards the glorious freedom of the children of God.[87]

Man is not to demand that God inform him of His plans in the same manner that a soldier does not demand that his general reveal to him strategic military plans; or a student ask his teacher for the answers to the examination questions; or a card player to be shown the cards of a fellow player.

He Speaks to Us from Behind a Veil

Blessed John Henry Cardinal Newman, in a letter to the Duke of Norfolk, wrote: "Conscience is a messenger of Him who, both in nature and in grace, speaks to us behind the veil, and teaches and rules us by His representatives."[88] Although our Creator hides behind a veil, His voice speaks in our consciences. He is not a policeman; He is a loving Father who bends towards us in astonishing solicitude. He not only looks at us; He also listens to us lovingly all the time, even when it might appear otherwise. Clearly, directly, and gently, He speaks in varied and mysterious ways: through visions and locutions, with subtle clues, and through the events and circumstances of ordinary life.

Bishop Javier Echevarría said:

We can discover that Christ, hiding in the sacramental species, ... also fits in with God's express desire not to

---

[87] *Christ Is Passing By*, no. 130.
[88] John Henry Newman, *Letters to the Duke of Norfolk* (London: Longmans, Green, 1885), 248.

force human freedom. By hiding Himself, our Lord invites us to seek Him, while He puts Himself in our way; He comes out to meet us. How often this happened to St. Josemaría, who, without realizing it, without specifically seeking it, found himself "mulling over" words of Scripture that shed light on aspects of his work, showed him the will of God, and answered problems and doubts which he had put to his Lord![89]

The invisible Lord has placed the dividing barrier, and He crosses it whenever He wants with sovereign lordship and divine right. He does so when He grants supernatural graces, graces that come with the obligation to correspond with greater effort, for more is asked of those to whom more is given.

The dealings of God with every soul do not follow any fixed pattern: "The Spirit blows where it will" (see John 3:8). He manifests Himself suddenly, perhaps after a long period of silence and hiding. Such are His ways.

His Concealment Is Unannounced

I was surprised to find out, with the computer's help, that in the entire Bible, the expression "hidden God" appears only once: "Truly you are a hidden God, the God of Israel the Savior" (see Isa. 45:15). It was disappointing, for I had wished to search Scripture deeply about God's hiddenness and expected to find abundant references to it.

But it makes sense that God does not declare His concealment insistently: no one hiding announces himself. His hiddenness is

[89] Javier Echevarría, Pastoral Letter, October 6, 2004.

something for us to recognize, a discovery of faith that requires God's help and our free effort.

Love, Not Force

In any conversion, love is the main force at work. The shielded Lover goes after His offspring all the time. Since love is not to be imposed on anyone, He does no violence to the liberty He has gratuitously granted. God does not barge into souls even if He has the right to do so. He never forces anyone; He only offers and invites.

When Our Lady, the angels, and the saints obtain graces from God for our benefit, they do so in a way that could be characterized as discreet. In the favors obtained through the intercession of saints, God acts "discreetly" too by "leaving behind a door open." In this way, if someone refuses to believe in the intercession of the saints, he can attribute the favor to coincidence.

In accordance with God's manner of acting, the persons of the transcendent world follow the ways of the Master when they refrain from violating a rule of the subtle Lord — to respect human freedom by remaining unseen.

Two Perspectives

The veiled Overseer warned us, "My thoughts are not your thoughts, neither are your ways my ways. . . . For as the heavens are higher than the earth, so are my ways higher than your ways" (Isa. 55:8–9). Ernesto Juliá refers to the abyss between God's mind and ours in the following passage:

> God does not observe the historical human happenings the way we do. We know His plans of creation, redemption,

sanctification of man, the "whole" man, and "all" of men; but we do not know His mind in the development of these plans, nor the divine way of progressively unveiling throughout human history, the unfathomable richness hidden in Christ Jesus.[90]

As human history unfolded, the covered Lover is shown to have removed in varied forms the veil that hides Him from our view—though never in the overwhelming manner reserved for the Second Coming, which will be the climax of the unveiling process. The ultimate disclosure will be the vision of the Lord that all the elect in Heaven will enjoy eternally.

Until this final disclosure occurs—to use a favorite expression of St. Josemaría—we ought to accept that we do not understand His ways. The reason is simple: His mind is infinite, and ours is limited. To recognize this fact is a sign of authentic humility, for it is the plain truth; and "humility," St. Teresa of Jesus loved to say, is "to walk in truth." We just bow our heads and accustom ourselves to the state of affairs. Any demand that God give understanding of why things happen in a particular way is arrogance toward Him, who "opposes the proud, but gives grace to the humble" (1 Pet. 5:5).

---

[90] Ernesto Juliá, *Josemaría Escrivá: Vivencias y recuerdos* (Madrid: Palabra, 2002), 21.

7

God's Test

I was delighted every day, playing before him at all times.
—Proverbs 8:30, Douay-Rheims

God involves mankind in an important game, in which everyone has to take part. It consists in seeking, finding, adoring, and loving God, and helping others to do the same. Participation in the game is not optional. Some engage in it willingly, others less so. Others choose to default.

God is the infinite Organizer, Player, and Referee, and human beings are the finite contestants, who, although totally disadvantaged, still feel the immense honor of being called to play. The stakes are high: eternal happiness or eternal damnation.

There are in nature other creatures of the mineral, vegetable, and animal realms, but the Lord does not play with them, nor are they tested. Their existence is predetermined and fixed. They are deprived of the excitement, joy, and adventure of the transcendent game, which leads men to thank God for the precious gift of freedom—a requisite for playing.

God wants His offspring to experience, guided by reason and faith, the thrill of looking for Him and savoring the great joy of finding Him. This joy is imperfect for now, because even after we "find" Him, the concealed One remains veiled. Not until the Last Day will everything be made manifest and clear as daylight. Then and only then will the game be over.

The happiness a person experiences when he sees God's hand behind events confirms that joy and excitement as well as sorrow and pain are "part of the game" of life. Anyone who finds all these considerations somewhat childish need only recall the words of Jesus Christ: "Truly, I say to you, unless you ... become like children, you will never enter the kingdom of heaven" (Matt. 18:3).

This is how the founder of Opus Dei envisioned it:

If the thought ever passes through our minds, in the face of effort or dryness, that we are "play-acting," our reaction should be to think that the wonderful moment has come to perform a human play for a divine spectator: the Father, the Son, and the Holy Spirit, the Blessed Trinity. And together with God our Lord, the Mother of God and the angels and saints will also be watching us.

We cannot abandon a life of piety, our life of sacrifice and love. When we act out a play for God, for love of Him, trying to please Him; when we go "against the grain"; when we feel we are playing the role of a jester: let us think that we are jesters of God. It's a beautiful thing—never doubt it—to perform a play for Love, sacrificing ourselves, without any personal reward, simply to please God who is playing with us.[91]

---

[91] St. Josemaría Escrivá, Letter, March 24, 1931, 18–19.

God's Test

The Rules of the Game

There are a number of rules that, from man's perspective, govern this game. The relationship with the Almighty is characterized by the following set of *unwritten rules*:

1. Life on earth is fundamentally a test and a game of faith.

2. The Lord is veiled by His own design. He created and brought human beings into existence for this test and game in order to grant them the immense opportunity of eternal happiness.

3. Participation is not optional. Ignoring and rejecting the call to play are in themselves ways of participating.

4. The game can be played only once, and no one can play for another.

5. The divine Lover gives self-determination to the participants. This respect for freedom might be called "the golden rule of the hidden God."

6. Accordingly, the freedom of one's fellow men must be respected.

7. Players shall not sin against the light! Translation: They must be honest with themselves, with others, and with God. They are to be coherent with themselves and His Truth. It is one thing to misbehave because light is lacking, and another to brush aside the light. There will always be enough light for those who want to believe and enough darkness for those who do not.

8. Complaints or sadness while seeking the Father are forbidden. It does not make sense to be gloomy while one advances toward a ravishing eternal enjoyment.

9. The time of trial is a walk in the shadows, and this is part of the game. God said: "Man shall not see me and live" (Exod. 33:20). Absolute clarity can be found only at the end of the game.

10. God may not be "put on the spot" by our asking Him to work miracles, as Satan did in the desert. The Lord will not submit Himself to the arrogant test of anyone.

11. Yet He listens to all the requests of the humble and the faithful, in mysterious ways.

12. Requests have to be made humbly. To ask why or to demand an answer is futile and arrogant: Life on earth is not a problem to be solved, but a mystery to accept, with faith.

13. He knows best! For He has said: "My thoughts are not your thoughts, neither are your ways my ways.... For as the heavens are higher than the earth, so are my ways higher than your ways."

14. Neither may His plans be demanded of Him. In the universal test and game, players are called to accept and abide by the rules.

15. Interpreting the meaning of the clues God sends is part of the communication with Him, an art that needs to be learned.

16. In this game, it is wise to take risks, as long as it is done under the light of prudence. The more faith and hope and love there is, the better.

17. Death and judgment will also mark the end of the game for the individual. For the whole of mankind, the

end of the test and game will come with the Second Coming.

18. The human players' task is to figure out the above *unwritten rules* and abide by them.

20. God is the Organizer and the main Player of this game. There is no higher court to appeal to. His mercy and His love for everyone are infinite. All the Father God does and permits — including some very hard challenges of the game — is for the good and happiness of His children.

8

At the End of the Game

⸺ ❀ ⸺

*The crucible is for silver, and the furnace is
for gold, and the LORD tries hearts.*

—Proverbs 17:3

In the attempt to gain insight into the mystery of the veiled God,
we considered the situation of mankind in relation to Him. We
compared the present days to a test given by the Divine Proctor,
who, in order to not overwhelm us with His presence, and to
leave us completely free, is hiding, as it were, in a balcony from
which He sees His offspring, in their inner and external being,
with perfect clarity.

Our earthly journey is a real, though mysterious, trial. Our
entire conscious life is continuously being tested. For instance,
when things are going well for us, the Lord observes whether we
give Him thanks and due credit for the success. When things go
badly, He expects a prayer for His help.

Meanwhile, God wants His creatures' lives to be tension-free
as He watches them every moment, and that is one of the reasons
He hides. He is a withdrawn paternal Examiner. He cares and
loves infinitely.

Fundamentally, this life is a test of Faith to which everyone is called. Many things that come about during this period of assessment are beyond our understanding. It will always be like that until the end of time.

In Sacred Scripture, there are many instances in which God tests people. According to Christian tradition, the angels were the first to be subjected to a trial, followed by the test of Adam and Eve:

> Now the serpent was subtler than any other wild creature that the LORD God had made. He said to the woman, "Did God say, 'You shall not eat of any tree of the garden'?" And the woman said to the serpent, "We may eat of the fruit of the trees of the garden; but God said, 'You shall not eat of the fruit of the tree which is in the midst of the garden, neither shall you touch it, lest you die.'" (Gen. 3:1–3).

This was the first test for human beings. Subsequently, all descendants of Adam and Eve, without exception, are tried. In some cases, the testing is dramatic. The Lord permitted Job to be severely tempted by Satan to the point at which the patriarch exclaimed in extreme anxiety: "The arrows of the Almighty are in me; my spirit drinks their poison; the terrors of God are arrayed against me" (Job 6:4).

In the New Testament, God continues probing individuals. Christ allowed Himself to be tempted. According to the Gospel of St. Matthew: "Jesus was led up by the Spirit into the wilderness to be tempted by the devil" (Matt. 4:1). Jesus is the Light of the world. Yet even after the Messiah's coming, God remained a veiled God. He came to give us the opportunity to be blessed and happy without touching Him, as the Apostle Thomas needed to do to believe in Him.

Wayfarers encounter lights that are bright and shadows that may be awfully dark. It is the chiaroscuro of the human condition, where there will always be enough light for those who want to believe, and enough darkness for those who refuse to do so. Nonetheless, this is not meant to last forever. When Jesus comes to earth the second time, all the shadows will vanish, and what Christ meant when He said: "I am the light of the world" (John 9:5) will be fully manifested.

St. Paul instructs us regarding Christ's Second Coming: "When Christ who is our life appears, then you also will appear with him in glory" (Col. 3:4). The Second Coming of Jesus will be the culmination and the end of all tests and of the coexistence of light and darkness; and, for those who are saved, it will mark the beginning of everlasting light in soul and body.

Light from the First Pope

Much light can be gleaned from the first letter of St. Peter, who wrote: "By God's power [you] are guarded through faith for a salvation ready to be revealed in the last time" (1 Pet. 1:5). St. Peter equates salvation with the revelation to come, referring to the remuneration that will come to both body and soul in His Second Coming. He explains:

> In this you rejoice, though now for a little while you may have to suffer various trials, so that the genuineness of your faith, more precious than gold which though perishable is tested by fire, may redound to praise and glory and honor at the revelation of Jesus Christ. Without having

seen him you love him; though you do not now see him
you believe in him and rejoice with unutterable and
exalted joy. As the outcome of your faith you obtain the
salvation of your souls.... [Christ] was destined before the
foundation of the world but was made manifest at the end
of times for your sake. (1 Pet. 1:6–9, 20)

Judgment

It is shattering to read the following words in the Gospel after
Jesus cured a blind man:

> "For judgment I came into this world, that those who
> do not see may see, and that those who see may become
> blind."[40] Some of the Pharisees near him heard this, and
> they said to him, "Are we also blind?"[41] Jesus said to them,
> "If you were blind, you would have no guilt; but now that
> you say, 'We see,' your guilt remains." (John 9:39–41)

There is such a thing as voluntary and culpable blindness, and
one of the main tenets of these pages is that our life is first and
foremost a test of faith.

How can anyone be frivolous with the thought of the existence
of Hell? Dale Ahlquist wrote:

> While the fear of death is universal, the fear of damnation
> is more personal, more individual, because the fear
> of damnation is the voice of our conscience. It is the
> inescapable sense that if we were to get the judgement
> that we really deserved, it would not be pretty. Justice
> is something we all want when we feel we have been
> wronged. But justice is something we really don't like to

think about the rest of the time, which is most of the time. Our fear of damnation is really only a deep realization that God is just. They [unbelievers] have forgotten God certainly. But their big mistake before that was that they had forgotten hell. When you forget hell ... you have collapsed into egoism and self-centeredness. Hell is separation from God. And just to make it worse, hell is being stuck with only yourself.[92]

When the Test Is Over

A rule of the universal game comes from the Almighty's words "For man shall not see me and live!" The Lord does not want the great barrier that separates this life from the next to be breached. It is different when the test is over; then there will be "a new heaven and a new earth."

As the Filipino theologian Joselito Jose Alviar envisions it:

In the *escathon,* the universe will reach its supreme *sacramental* form (sign), leaving behind its *veiling* dimension of God's presence. It will keep only its manifesting function: it will make manifest God's presence (all in all). Thus, the cosmos, as is the case of the risen man, will be at last a great souvenir or manifestation of God's glory, an extension of Christ, the primordial sacrament, a place of God's presence, house of God, and an eschatological temple.[93]

---

[92] Dale Ahlquist, "A Happy Little Reflection on Hell," *The Catholic Servant* (2011).

[93] Joselito Jose Alviar, *Escatologia* (Spain: EUNSA, 2004), 189.

Alviar points to the veiling function of the world because the universe is marked with the cosmic consequences of sin as well as the challenges to belief in a benevolent Maker. It is also the setting for the test that everyone is taking. Later, it will be different. The test will be over, and the splendid and permanent prize for the saved will be the ecstatic enjoyment of eternal union with God.

In Heaven all is clarity; in Hell all is darkness, but the present test is a mixture of light and shadow. One day, when sister death comes, the silent Maker will no longer be silent. He will utter the decisive word, and everyone will pass from the noisy world to the other world. There, for the saved, everything to be said will just be in one Word: the *Verbum*, the *Logos*. There is no need for any other.

Then, as Christ said to His disciples, "Nothing is covered that will not be revealed, or hidden that will not be known" (Matt. 10:26).

9

Faith, Freedom, and Love

Blessed are those who have not seen and yet believe.

—John 20:29

Faith plays a pivotal part in man's relations with the veiled Lord. It is the most fundamental subject matter of the test men take on earth, for they cannot love or hope in someone they do not believe in. That is why no atheist loves God, or hopes in Him. The Council of Trent stated that "faith is the beginning, the foundation, and the root of justification, and without faith it is impossible to please God and to be numbered among His sons."[94]

Faith is a condition for all successful dealings with the concealed Father. For all prayers of petition, the amount of faith in God's power is important, for He Himself said: "Whatever you ask in prayer, you will receive, if you have faith" (Matt. 21:22). When Simon Peter was sinking in the lake of Galilee, Jesus reached out his hand and caught him saying: "O man of little faith, why did you doubt?" (Matt. 14:31).

---

[94] Session VI, Decree on Justification, chap. 8.

In the words of Pope Francis, "Faith is born of an encounter with the living God, who calls us and reveals His love, a love that precedes us."[95] He added:

> In God's gift of faith, a supernatural infused virtue, we realize that a great love has been offered us, a good word has been spoken to us, and that when we welcome that word, Jesus Christ, the Word made flesh, the Holy Spirit transforms us, lights up our way to the future, and enables us joyfully to advance along the way on wings of hope.[96]

Benedict XVI explained it this way:

> The "door of faith" (Acts 14:27) is always open to us, ushering us into the life of communion with God and offering entry into his Church. It is possible to cross that threshold when the word of God is proclaimed, and the heart allows itself to be shaped by transforming grace.[97]

The giving of assent, the Holy Father added, implies free acceptance of the whole mystery of faith because the guarantor of its truth is God, who reveals Himself and allows us to know His mystery of love. He continued:

> On the other hand, we must not forget that in our cultural context, very many people, while not claiming to have the gift of faith, are nevertheless sincerely searching for the ultimate meaning and definitive truth of their lives

---

[95] Pope Francis, Encyclical Letter *Lumen Fidei* (June 29, 2013), no. 4.

[96] Ibid., no. 7.

[97] Benedict XVI, Apostolic Letter *Porta Fidei* (October 11, 2011), no. 1.

and of the world. This search is an authentic "preamble" to the faith because it guides people onto the path that leads to the mystery of God. Human reason, in fact, bears within itself a demand for "what is perennially valid and lasting." This demand constitutes a permanent summons, indelibly written in the human heart, to set out to meet the one whom we would not be seeking had He not already set out to meet us. To this encounter, faith invites us and it opens us in fullness.[98]

These words of Pope Benedict XVI show that the initiative in the act of faith belongs to God. As Cardinal Leo Scheffczyk, referring to the true nature of faith, pointed out:

[Christianity's] essence is not as abstract and theoretical as are the fundamental tenets of a philosophical system. This misunderstanding must be countered by the truth that the Christian faith constitutes most deeply the encounter with Christ and the participation in his Person, "so that Christ may live in your hearts through faith" (Eph. 3:17). However, Christ was himself the first witness to faith. Because he was the first "faithful witness" to faith (Rev. 1:5; 3:15) and because Christians are vitally connected to this witness, their faith must become expressed by confession as well as by witnessing. The confession is not the result of an afterthought — that is, a positivistic instruction — but it evolves out of the unity with Christ and culminates in martyrdom.[99]

---

[98] Ibid., no. 10.

[99] Leo Scheffczyk, "Faith and Witness: Confesio and martyrium," *Communio International Catholic Review* 22, no. 3 (Fall 1995).

Pope Francis further explained that, "in faith, Christ is not simply the one in whom we believe, the supreme manifestation of God's love; He is also the one with whom we are united precisely to believe."[100] And also: "Faith without truth does not save; it does not provide a sure footing."[101]

Together with faith, a humble attitude is necessary to discover the Lord, for "God opposes the proud, but gives grace to the humble" (James 4:6). Those blinded by their egotism, self-admiration, and self-worship are not capable even of recognizing the truth of their lives.

Those who realize their sinfulness and need help, the humble, are those whom the Holy Spirit assists and enables to discover the silent Father. To receive the grace of faith, a proper preparation of the intellect and of the will is needed. It is the Holy Spirit's task to move the will, to enlighten the intellect, and to enkindle the heart.

Faith and the Signs

There is ample evidence in the Gospels of how much Jesus suffered on encountering lack of faith. He continuously strove to lift the people's outlook from the natural to the supernatural level, but He did not always succeed. Once He complained, "You search the scriptures, because you think that in them you have eternal life; and it is they that bear witness to me" (John 5:39). After the multiplication of the loaves, He said, "You seek me, not because you saw signs, but because you ate your fill of the loaves. Do not labor for the food which perishes, but for the

[100] Francis, *Lumen Fidei*, no. 18.
[101] Ibid., no. 24.

food which endures to eternal life, which the Son of man will give to you" (John 6:26–27).

Many of those who witnessed Jesus' miracles admired the prodigies but failed to take them as signs and proofs of His divinity. Jesus worked many miracles; Judas witnessed many of them, yet he did not believe deeply enough. Miracles are not sufficient to guarantee the fidelity of anyone.

Faith allows the reading of facts as signs of something supernatural. Without it, we would always remain on the natural plane, unable to climb, totally blind to the supernatural world. Pope Francis explained it this way: "Those who believe see; they see with a light that illumines their entire journey, for it comes from the risen Christ, the morning star which never sets."[102]

"In Tabor," wrote Bishop Javier Echevarría, "there was light from God that came from above. In the Eucharist, there is the light that comes from down, from us: It is the light of our Faith given to us by God."[103]

Good Dispositions

How touching it is to see the Almighty God hiding as if He were a fugitive! The Gospel of St. John reads: "When Jesus had said this, he departed and hid himself from them. Though he had done so many signs before them, yet they did not believe in him" (John 12:36–37). These words point out the tremendous duty to respond to the Lord's gifts. Those who see signs are gifted by the Almighty, who expects faith, trust, and love in return. If, in spite of the lights, men persist in refusing to believe, they

---

[102] Francis, *Lumen Fidei*, no. 1.
[103] Javier Echevarría, Pastoral Letter, January 1, 2005.

greatly offend Him, for they have sinned against the light. They can no longer say that they act in good faith. The Almighty has extended His hand, but they reject it, for they have blinded themselves.

Prayer and Faith

Human beings find themselves separated from the "cloud of witnesses" by a barrier that only faith can penetrate, in the manner that x-rays pass through flesh and reveal bones. Prayer establishes contact with the three Divine Persons and with the other persons of the supernatural world: the Blessed Mother, St. Joseph, the angels and saints, the souls in Purgatory—all of whom, like the Almighty, are unseen. Prayer can be described as the soul's contact with the persons who constitute the immense cloud of witnesses.

The purpose of every creature is to give glory to the Creator, to make His perfections manifest. Glory is given to the Lord only when he is discovered and personally encountered. Pope Benedict XVI wrote: "As we contemplate in the Mother of God a life totally shaped by the Word, we realize that we too are called to enter into the mystery of faith whereby Christ comes to dwell in our lives."[104]

As Dr. Francis Collins, the head of the Genome Project, puts it:

Prayer is not, as some seem to suggest, an opportunity to manipulate God into doing what you want Him to

---

[104] Benedict XVI, Apostolic Exhortation *Verbum Domini* (September 30, 2010), no. 28.

do. Prayer is instead our way of seeking fellowship with God, learning about Him, and attempting to perceive His perspective on the many issues around us that cause us puzzlement, wonder, or distress.[105]

Conviction and the Veil

Jesus said to the father of a possessed boy: "All things are possible to him who believes" (Mark 9:23). Among these things is the power to pierce the veil that covers the supernatural world.

Every time a person prays the Our Father, the Hail Mary, or any prayer with conviction, with faith, the barrier separating men from the invisible world is lifted. And the greater the conviction, the greater the faith, the deeper the veil is entered, the closer one can get to Him. Merit and demerit depend on the degree of awareness and the control of the situation.

God is veiled. This is the cause of man's deepest existential anguish. But He has graciously left clues that point not only to His existence as a Creator, but to His fatherly care and determination to save us through His Son. Chief among these signs are the Church and, through her, the sacraments and her teachings.

The Eyes of Faith

There is the sad possibility of searching for the Almighty among material things. When the Russian astronaut Gherman Titov returned from outer space, he made the infamous comment that he was disappointed for "not having found God up there." It is

---

[105] Francis S. Collins, *The Language of God* (New York: Free Press, 2006), 220.

not a surprising comment, for only by a mind open to spiritual realities can God be found.

Man's entire life is a test of faith. If he wants, he can see, since there is infinite light. To use a favorite expression of St. Josemaría, "It is a matter of faith."

God invites us to look for Him: "For God so loved the world that he gave his only Son, that whoever believes in him should not perish but shall have eternal life. For God sent his Son into the world, not to condemn the world, but that the world might be saved through him. He who believes in him is not condemned; he who does not believe is condemned already, because he has not believed in the name of the only Son of God" (John 3:16–18). Since faith is necessary for salvation, the eternal Father will not deny it to anyone. No one can excuse a lack of effort or interest by saying that he has not received the gift of faith. The Constitution *Dei Verbum* stated, "Revelation is the fruit of His goodness and of His wisdom."[106] And since the Almighty is infinitely good, He will never deny anyone sufficient help to attain salvation. On the other hand, as Pope Francis taught, "One who believes may not be presumptuous; on the contrary, truth leads to humility, since believers know that rather than ourselves possessing the truth, it is the truth which embraces and possesses us."[107]

A Matter of Faith

In *Deus Caritas Est*, Pope Benedict XVI describes the present earthly situation together with the fundamental role faith plays:

---

[106] Second Vatican Council, Dogmatic Constitution on Divine Revelation *Dei Verbum* (November 18, 1965), no. 2.
[107] Francis, *Lumen Fidei*, no. 34.

Christians continue believing, in spite of all the lack of understanding and confusion obtaining in the world around them, in the "goodness of God and the love of man" (Titus 3:4). Even though they are immersed as other men are in dramatic and complex historical vicissitudes, they remain firm in the certitude that God is Father and loves us, in spite of the fact that His silence continues being incomprehensible to us.[108]

In *Porta Fidei*, the now Pope Emeritus says:

St. Luke recounts that, while he was at Philippi, Paul went on the Sabbath to proclaim the Gospel to some women; among them was Lydia, and "the Lord opened her heart to give heed to what was said by Paul" (Acts 16:14). There is an important meaning contained within this expression. St. Luke teaches that knowing the content of faith is not sufficient, unless the heart, the authentic sacred space within the person, is opened by the grace that allows the eyes to see below the surface and to understand that what has been proclaimed is the word of God.[109]

The book of Wisdom perfectly explains the situation: "He is found by those who do not put him to the test, and manifests himself to those who do not distrust him" (1:2). St. Paul explains the human earthly condition in his Second Letter to the Corinthians:

Even if our gospel is veiled, it is veiled only to those who are perishing. In their case, the God of this world has

---

[108] Benedict XVI, *Deus Caritas Est*, no. 38.
[109] Benedict XVI, *Porta Fidei*, no. 10.

blinded the minds of the unbelievers, to keep them from seeing the light of the gospel of the glory of Christ, who is the likeness of God (4:3–4).

Worthwhile

To think for a fleeting moment about the things of Heaven is not difficult. To dwell calmly and lengthily on them is difficult. It is an exercise in faith, hope, and love. Contemplating the supernatural realities is an excellent source of peace and consolation.

The effort is worthwhile for man's eternal destiny. The pilgrimage of faith on earth is a path toward the vision in Heaven. As Michael Figura said:

> There is in man a yearning for salvation that is insatiable. This is connected with the fact that in man there is a natural desire for transcendence, which is fulfilled in the vision of God.... This longing can be stilled only by God. In the sending of His Son, God made known to us that He himself wants to be our salvation. Therefore, salvation for us consists in our entering into the loving and obedient relationship of Jesus to His Father, in our being children of God through the Spirit, in our having peace and friendship with God, participating in His life and becoming sharers in the divine life.[110]

---

[110] Michael Figura, "Faith as the Beginning of Salvation," *Communio International Catholic Review* 22, no. 3 (Fall 1995): 396.

Faith, Freedom, and Love

Faith Is the Finger

Once, a wise, young bishop[111] lamented that there are many in his midst who want to see, touch, and understand in order to believe. They have not discovered the richness of faith. The apostle Thomas was one of those who found it hard to believe. He needed to put his finger into the side of Jesus in order to believe. For us, explained the bishop, faith is the finger that enables us to touch the Lord, who is alive in our midst.

St. Teresa of Avila said something similar:

> Christ has no body but yours.
> No hands, no feet on earth but yours.
> Yours are the eyes with which He looks with
>   compassion on this world.
> Yours are the feet with which He walks to do good.
> Yours are the hands with which He blesses the
>   entire world.
> Yours are the hands, yours are the feet, and yours
>   are the eyes.
> You are His body.
> Christ has no body now but yours.

When Earth Joins Heaven

The concealed God lives in mystery. From the Christian's vantage point, He escapes sight, hearing, all the senses. The impression is that He is covered by a thick, impenetrable veil. And yet, while "living in the heights," He has found the way to reach out in many ways. He makes His existence and many of His perfections

---

[111] Romà Casanova, bishop of Vic (Barcelona) since June 13, 2003.

accessible to men's minds. A whole panorama of divine marvels has been made accessible with the gift of faith. One is the Holy Mass. In it, He unites Heaven and earth in a striking way. Vatican II explains it thus:

> In the earthly liturgy, we take part in a foretaste of that heavenly liturgy which is celebrated in the Holy City of Jerusalem toward which we journey as pilgrims, where Christ is sitting at the right hand of God, sanctuary minister of the holies and of the true tabernacle.[112]

Divine Providence

Jacques Philippe points out that until the Lord's providence is experienced, it is hard to believe and abandon oneself to it.[113] He adds that we are blinded; we do not find Jesus' words good enough; in order to believe, we want to see at least a bit! But since we do not see it acting clearly among us, how could we experience it? We will experience God's help only if we allow Him the space to manifest Himself.

Philippe makes a comparison: as long as a parachutist does not jump into the air, he cannot verify the support of the ropes. He needs to jump first, and only then will he feel supported. In the spiritual life, the same thing happens: "God gives to the extent that we hope in Him," says St. John of the Cross. St. Francis de Sales adds:

---

[112] Second Vatican Council, Constitution on the Sacred Liturgy *Sacrosanctum Concilium* (December 4, 1963), no. 8.

[113] Jacques Philippe, *La paz interior* (Madrid: Ediciones Rialp, S.A., 2004), 31.

The measure of Divine Providence towards us is the trust we have in it. This is the root of the problem: many do not believe in Providence because they have never experienced it, but they have not experienced it because they have never taken the jump in the air, the jump of faith, and thus, they have not given Him the possibility to intervene.[114]

To trust Divine Providence is to trust the unseen Father, who is pleased with this trust. St. Teresa of Jesus said: "The most wretched person is the one who hears God's voice but cannot break away from worldly things."

According to Dr. Francis Collins:

If the case in favor of belief in God were utterly airtight, then the world would be full of confident practitioners of a single faith. But imagine such a world, where the opportunity to make a free choice about belief was taken away by the certainty of the evidence. How interesting would that be?[115]

Not only would it not be interesting; it would cease being the most important test that exists. Benedict XVI teaches that, "When we believe, we freely accept the whole mystery of faith because the guarantor of its truth is God who reveals Himself and allows us to know His mystery of love."[116]

Some people feel uncomfortable flying in a plane. They feel at ease only when the aircraft has landed because they are not creatures of the sky. In the life of faith, taking off from the ground toward the supernatural does not bring uneasiness because everyone

[114] Ibid., 32.
[115] Collins, *The Language of God*, 33–34.
[116] Benedict XVI, *Porta Fidei*, no. 10.

is called to be a *dual citizen* of the natural and the supernatural worlds.

Truths that are obscure bring disquiet to the intellect, which is always keen to understand everything that is geared to the truth. Faith infuses a great light in the intellect. The Church that Christ founded has always rejoiced in her Faith, yet "there are some who pass through life as through a tunnel: they fail to realize the splendor and the security and the warmth of the sun of faith."[117]

Msgr. Pedro Rodriguez described the effects of the sun of faith in men and women of God:

We have all known, and know, persons whose lives we admire. Their dedication to the things of God is so great and so natural that when we are with them, we have the impression of being closer to the Lord; we see them so united to God that we would say that they touch Him, that they see Him. When they speak to us about God, their conversation is not "of a book," but fruit of their experience of divine things. For them, faith and its contents are fountains of knowledge, light that fecundates their spirit and makes them penetrate God's mystery.... This "communion" with God that faith produces is a fruit of our identification through love with the witness which gives us certitude.[118]

How powerful the rays of faith are! They have more penetrating power than x-rays. They allow us to *see* the Risen Christ in the

---

[117] St. Josemaría Escrivá, *The Way*, no. 575.

[118] Pedro Rodríguez, *La fe como conocimiento de Dios* (Spain: EUNSA, 1974), 105–106.

tabernacle, in other people, and behind the events of everyday life.

Conversely, the lack of faith elicits concern. This is how St. Josemaría put it:

> I must confide to you something which makes me suffer and spurs me on to action: the thought of all those people who do not yet know Christ, who do not even suspect the great good fortune which awaits us in heaven. They live like blind men looking for a joy whose real name they don't know, lost on roads which take them away from true happiness.[119]

Faith and hope come and go together. To rely on the veiled Father is a manifestation of faith as much as of hope, and others can notice the effects of these virtues: "You were pessimistic, hesitant, and apathetic. Now you are completely transformed: you feel courageous, optimistic, and self-confident, because you have made up your mind, at last, to rely on God alone," was St. Josemaría's observation.

The End Times

We are in the end times — that is, the period between the Annunciation and the Second Coming. The manifestation of the Word made flesh, the Incarnation, requires faith, for it is not yet the perfect manifestation to be enjoyed in the Beatific Vision. This is why some did not believe in Jesus in spite of the miracles He performed. The coming of Christ does not deprive anyone of the merit of faith, although it facilitates very much the

---

[119] Josemaría Escrivá, *Christ Is Passing By*, no. 173.

relationship with the Almighty God. Out of His great love, He suspended His policy of concealment and, with the Incarnation, took a giant leap toward self-manifestation.

Right after Adam's expulsion from Paradise, Yahweh cloaked Himself from human perception. However, by the gift of the patriarchs, such as Noah, Abraham, and Moses, and the prophets, such as Elijah, Jeremiah, and Isaiah, He began showing Himself more clearly and closely. The fullness of time arrived with Christ, and with Him was achieved the maximum illumination experienced in the present exile. "I am the light of the world," He said. "He who follows me will not walk in darkness but will have the light of life" (John 8:12).

The book of Exodus records a dialogue between Yahweh and Moses that is very telling:

> And the LORD said to Moses, "This very thing that you have spoken I will do; for you have found favor in my sight, and I know you by name." Moses said, "I pray thee, show me thy glory." And he said, "I will make all my goodness pass before you and will proclaim before you my name 'The Lord.' ... But," he said, "you cannot see my face; for man shall not see me and live" (Exod. 33:17–20).

Moses' eagerness to see Yahweh face-to-face is the universal aspiration of every human being on earth. This desire is intense and deeply ingrained because it is man's ultimate destiny, his final calling, and exactly what God had wanted him to enjoy forever. At the same time, these verses from the book of Exodus make clear that the present time is not meant to be spent in an insistent pursuit of a face-to-face vision of the Lord, but rather as a pilgrimage of faith.

Faith, Freedom, and Love

Freedom Defined

Pope John Paul II felt indebted to St. Thomas Aquinas for a precise definition of what constitutes man's greatness: "He has charge of himself."[120] Man is master of himself; he can make provision for himself and form projects toward fulfilling his destiny. The decisive factor is that man should let truth guide him in his actions. But man does not make truth; he can only discover it.

The freedom with which the Creator endowed man is the capacity to seek what is true by using his intelligence, and to embrace the good to which he naturally aspires, without being subjected to pressures, constraints, or violence. It belongs to the dignity of the person to respond to the moral imperative of his conscience in the search for truth. The truth, as the Second Vatican Council emphasized, "is to be sought after in a manner proper to the dignity of the human person and his social nature"[121] and cannot impose itself except by virtue of its own truth.

Conscience is free and ought not to be violated. God Himself respects the freedom of the human person. But man is obligated to form a right conscience by learning the law. He cannot neglect this responsibility without committing sin. Man's conscience is not above the law. The distinguished jurist Cormac Burke remarks:

> Conscience is a precious but delicate guide. Its voice is easily distorted or obscured. To dictate to the conscience is to silence, and eventually to destroy it. Conscience

---

[120] "*Ipse est sibi providens.*" St. Thomas Aquinas, *Summa Contra Gentiles*, bk. 3, chap. 81.

[121] Second Vatican Council, Declaration on Religious Freedom *Dignitatis Humanae* (December 7, 1965), no. 3.

must be listened to and listened to sensitively. It needs to be interrogated, even to be cross-examined. And only those who habitually interrogate their conscience and are ready to pay heed, even to its awkward answers, will not cheat their conscience or be cheated by it.

Freedom, Reward, Punishment

The Almighty's fatherly love manifests itself in His eagerness to compensate Christians with the gift of eternal union with Him. Since this prize is immense, the Lord wants a token of the willingness to cooperate with His plan. Now, in order to do anything meritorious, man must be free. An animal or a machine could be engaged for many hours in useful activity without meriting anything because animals and machines have no freedom. But God gives man free will, which is inseparable from responsibility.[122] Consequently, man can receive recompense and punishment.

In this life, the Lord tests us on the love that follows faith. In an often-quoted passage, St. John of the Cross stated: "At the evening of our lives, we will be examined concerning love." "If we did not have the option of choosing sin and hell," says Scott Hahn, "we could not have the opportunity of truly choosing and loving God. If God did not permit us to say no to Him, our yes would be worthless, the programmed response of a machine.[123]

---

[122] It is well known that when G. K. Chesterton went to New York and saw at the port the famous statue of freedom, he remarked that there should be an equal at its side in honor of responsibility.

[123] Scott Hahn, Lord, Have Mercy! (New York: Doubleday, 2003), 90.

Faith, Freedom, and Love

Condemned to Freedom?

Jean-Paul Sartre's lament was "We are condemned to freedom!"[124] It is a striking lament, since from the perspective of faith, freedom is a great gift from the Maker, a meaningless yoke only to those who lose sight of liberty as the key to earn merit. Only because we are free can we expect any compensation at the end of life. This is how Deuteronomy presents it:

> See, I have set before you this day life and goodness, death and evil. If you obey the commandments of the LORD your God which I command you this day, by loving the LORD your God, by walking in his ways, and by keeping his commandments and his statutes and his ordinances, then you shall live.... Choose life, that you ... may live (Deut. 30:15–16, 19).

"Someone has compared the heart to a windmill moved by the wind of love and passion," wrote the founder of Opus Dei. "Indeed, that 'windmill' can grind wheat, barley, or dried dung. It is up to us."[125] The covered God has granted man the great gift of self-determination. It is up to man to make of it a blessing or a curse. "Only in freedom can man direct himself toward goodness."[126]

The Almighty will not suppress man's freedom because to do so would reduce persons to the state of brutes or slaves. He

---

[124] See Joseph M. de Torre, *Contemporary Philosophical Issues in Historical Perspective* (Manila: University of Asia and the Pacific, 2001), 91.

[125] Josemaría Escrivá, *Furrow* (Manila: Sinag-tala, 2000), no. 811.

[126] Second Vatican Council, Pastoral Constitution on the Church in the Modern Word *Gaudium et Spes* (December 7, 1965), no. 17.

cannot be blamed for the human evils that originate from the abuse of freedom, such as crimes, drug abuse, alcoholism, and other vices.

Wrote St. Josemaría, "The kingdom of Christ is a kingdom of freedom. In it the only slaves are those who freely bind themselves out of love of God. What a blessed slavery is love that sets us free!"[127] The best way of exercising our liberty is to put it totally at the Lord's disposal. Some philosophers call our will the rational appetite. Just as animal appetites are geared toward material goods, such as food, the will is directed toward goodness without limit. Therefore, to commit one's entire life to God, who is infinite Goodness, is the best and happiest choice one could make, as well as the most excellent possible exercise of free will.

St. Thomas Aquinas sees our will as the queen of all human faculties when it comes to operations and activity. He sees the intelligence as light, and the will with its self-determination as the motor of our actions. He sees both powers as open to infinity.

The Spanish archbishop Justo Mullor summarized his reflections on freedom saying: "My liberty extols me. My freedom weighs on me."

Luis M. Martinez, a distinguished Mexican prelate, explained: "It is our glory to fulfil our own destiny. God has given us the wonderful and terrible gift of freedom by which we ourselves are artisans of our own happiness, or our own ruin."[128]

The *Catechism of the Catholic Church* teaches: "As long as freedom has not bound itself definitively to its ultimate good which is God, there is the possibility of choosing between

---

[127] Josemaría Escrivá, *Christ Is Passing By*, no. 184.
[128] Luis M. Martinez, *True Devotion to the Holy Spirit* (Manchester: Sophia Institute Press, 2000), 128.

good and evil, and thus of growing in perfection, or failing and sinning" (no. 1732).

The Value of Freedom

Eberhard Schockenhoff wrote:

> The infinite power of God is shown in His making room for a finite freedom. The beginning of freedom is not a human auto-capacitation, but the initiative of the unlimited love of God, who is capable of doing the most elevated thing that He can do for a being, namely, to make him free.[129]

When we consider beasts of burden that work the fields all over the world, we say: "Poor animals! How much work and effort, and no recompense!" Why is this so? The answer is that they are not taking any transcendental test; they are just programmed from all eternity to do what they are doing. The Creator did not give them the gift of self-determination.

The human case is different. The test that men are subjected to is an assessment that lasts as long as responsible life lasts.

The following words of Bishop Javier Echevarría show the way the Lord deals with His children's freedom:

> He went to Gethsemane with His own, and asked them to accompany Him by telling them, "remain here" and later, "watch with me." In spite of their imperative form, these words were in reality requests, petitions. They were

---

[129] Quoted in Martin Schlag, "Theologie der Freiheit," *Scripta Theologica* 42, no. 2 (2010, Universidad de Navarra): 489.

a forceful way to express His human need for company, as well as the great need for the disciples to unite themselves to His prayer. There are no adequate words to describe the love of the Creator for freedom: He calls us to be witnesses of the marvelous richness of His life and of His interest in our salvation, but not even in these transcendental moments did He impose himself.... We Christians are to convince ourselves that our Lord does not cease to invite us to be at His side because He wishes to count on us and so that other souls will learn to follow Him, but He prefers that we decide to do so freely.[130]

The Lord prefers to act this way, for He wants to uphold the liberty of persons. It is moving to realize that even in the tragic moments of His Passion, the Lord refrains from imposing Himself. He wants not slaves but children who follow Him freely. Such is "glorious liberty of the children of God" (Rom. 8:21).

Very often, the miracles of Jesus were rewards for the faith shown by the beneficiaries. He did not want to force anyone into believing; this was not the purpose of His signs. They were for the benefit of people of goodwill. Many scriptural passages, such as the following one, make this evident:

And as Jesus passed on from there, two blind men followed him, crying aloud, "Have mercy on us, Son of David." When he entered the house, the blind men came to him; and Jesus said to them, "Do you believe that I am able to do this?" They said to him, "Yes, Lord." Then he touched their eyes, saying, "According to your faith

[130] Javier Echevarría, *Getsemani: En Oracion con Jesucristo* (Spain: Planeta, 2005), 15.

be it done to you." And their eyes were opened (Matt. 9:27–30).

Henry Bocala explains man's free relationship with the Lord:

God makes the first move and He draws us to Him. He crosses our path on purpose. But He never coerces us to believe "because the act of faith is of its very nature a free act" (*Catechism*, no. 160). In inviting us to assent, God can only do so much. The reality of man's freedom makes God's business risky.[131]

Vittorio Messori, who spent many years studying what he calls "the Mystery around us" states that

the God in whom Christians trust differs from any other, above all, by the fact that He is a God Who *proposes* that we would believe in Him. He is not a God who *imposes* the acceptance of the evidence of His existence and of His actuation in the world. He wants us to be His children, not His servants.[132]

Messori adds:

In faith there is certitude, but also challenge; necessity, but also freedom. Only a God Who proposes Himself through marks and signs, without imposing Himself with all His glory, can establish a relationship with His creatures instead of a forced dependence. And this conforms to the fact that God is Love, for can there be

[131] Henry Bocala, *Arise and Walk* (Manila: Paulines, 2009), 30.
[132] Vittorio Messori, *El gran milagro* (Madrid: Editorial Planeta, 1999), 49.

a friendship, or even a love, in which someone imposes himself on the other?[133]

The *Catechism* states: "Man's response to God by faith must be free, and therefore nobody is to be forced to embrace the faith against his will. The act of faith is, of its very nature, a free act" (no. 160).

The Lord shows great respect for the freedom He gives men. As Jean Guitton says:

> For Christians, God is necessarily discreet. He has placed an appearance of probability in the doubts concerning His existence. He has wrapped Himself in shadows so that the faith would be more ardent and undoubtedly, in order to have the right to forgive our rejecting it.[134]

Referring to the demonstrability of the Catholic Faith as the true religion, Alfonso Aguiló writes:

> It is one thing that something would be demonstrable, and another, very different, that it would be evident. Take into account that not all truths are demonstrable. And even less for someone who understands a demonstration as something indefectibly tied to experimental sciences.
>
> It is not very academic, but it serves us to understand each other, to say that things are as if God would not want to oblige us to believe. God upholds the dignity of the human person which He Himself has created, and man has to govern himself by his self-determination. God acts respecting human freedom that much. Besides, if it

---

[133] Ibid., 50.
[134] See ibid., 50.

were something as evident as sunlight, there would be no need to demonstrate anything.... If in the will there is a disposition contrary to belief, nobody surrenders when faced with a demonstration which is not totally evident (some even when facing evident ones). Faith is a gift of God, but at the same time, it is a free act. In order to believe there has to be a free decision of the will.[135]

The same author explains a characteristic of belief with these words:

There is much difference between being dogmatic and believing firmly in something. The dogmatic attitudes originate from "imposing" dogmas, not from "proposing" them. And the Church addresses men fully respecting their capacity of self-determination. The Church proposes; She does not impose anything.

To believe is a consequence of the natural search for the truth to which everyone should be committed. On the other hand, to be dogmatic — a caricature of respect for the dogmas — is what has led some people to fall into various fanaticisms throughout history. But it would be unjust to lay at the door of the dogmas the responsibility for actions or attitudes of which some individuals were the sole culprits.[136]

Dale Ahlquist has a similar explanation:

[135] Alfonso Aguiló, *Es la religión Cristiana la verdadera?* (Madrid: Ediciones Palabra, 2009), 113–114.
[136] Alfonso Aguiló, *Es razonable ser creyente?* (Madrid: Ediciones Palabra, 2004), 219.

We were made for heaven, but we are not forced to go there. Chesterton says that it is a fundamental dogma of the Catholic Faith "that all human beings, without any exception whatever, were specially made, were shaped and pointed like shining arrows, for the end of hitting the mark of Beatitude. But the shafts of those arrows," he says "are feathered with free will, and therefore throw the shadow of all the tragic possibilities of free will."[137]

A Venture and an Adventure

In a sermon, Blessed John Henry Newman told those present that if they do not venture anything for the Faith, they do not have faith at all. He explained that by "venture" he meant risking, sacrificing, abandoning everything to faith in God's word. Commenting on Christ's question to James and John, "Are you able to drink the cup that I am to drink?" and their answer, "We are able" (Matt. 20:22), Newman said:

> They asked for the gift of eternal life; and he told them, not that they should have it, but that they must venture for it.... Success and reward everlasting they will have who persevere unto the end. Doubt we cannot, that the ventures of all Christ's servants must be returned to them at the Last Day with abundant increase. This is a true saying—He returns far more than we lend to Him, and without fail. But speaking of individuals, no one knows for certain that he himself will persevere; yet everyone

[137] Ahlquist, "A Happy Little Reflection on Hell."

among us, to give himself even a chance of success at all, must make a venture....

If then faith be the essence of a Christian life, it follows that our duty lies in risking upon Christ's word what we have for what we have not, and doing so in a noble, generous way, not indeed rashly or lightly.

The cardinal concludes by asking, "What have we ventured for Christ?"[138]

Faith and Love

In *Porta Fidei*, Benedict XVI explains the relationship between faith and love:

Today, there is need for stronger ecclesial commitment to new evangelization in order to rediscover the joy of believing and the enthusiasm for communicating the faith. In rediscovering his love day by day, the missionary commitment of believers attains force and vigor that can never fade away. Faith grows when it is lived as an experience of love received and when it is communicated as an experience of grace and joy.[139]

---

[138] Cardinal J. H. Newman, *The Ventures of Faith* (New York: Scepter, 1981), 10, 14, 16.

[139] Benedict XVI, *Porta Fidei*, no. 7.

10

God's Recompense

Behold, I am coming soon, bringing my recompense,
to repay everyone for what he has done.

—Revelation 22:12

St. Paul's letter to the Philippians provides a clue regarding the Lord's concealment from those who journey on earth. "Therefore, my beloved, as you have always obeyed, so now, not only as in my presence but much more in my absence, work out your own salvation" (2:12). St. Paul wanted the Philippians to observe his commands, in his absence as much as in his presence. He knew that it was hard to follow indications while he was absent, but he also knew that it would have much more merit. The same happens in our relations with the Almighty. To this effect, He wants us to pass the test of faith, hope, and love in this life and to earn greater merit on account of His seclusion.

In Paradise, Adam and Eve dealt with Yahweh with some familiarity, and so their responsibility for not doing God's will was immense, as we can see by the consequences that followed. Now human beings have less responsibility than our first parents.

Why God Hides

The Prize

God is love, and all His actions, including His concealment, are out of love. It might appear paradoxical, but He does want to give us the greatest possible gift: Himself!

In the parable of the rich man and Lazarus, Jesus pointed out that the present life is not inconsequential:

> There was a rich man, who was clothed in purple and fine linen and who feasted sumptuously every day. And at his gate lay a poor man named Lazarus, full of sores, who desired to be fed with what fell from the rich man's table; moreover, the dogs came and licked his sores. The poor man died and was carried by the angels to Abraham's bosom. The rich man also died and was buried; and in Hades, being in torment, he lifted up his eyes, and saw Abraham far off and Lazarus in his bosom (Luke 16:19–23).

As we saw in an earlier chapter, this life is a test, and the joyful truth is that after the test, if we are faithful, there is a prize waiting, which will compensate for every hard or even tragic thing we had to go through on earth. This recompense is not only a vision of the Maker but a nuptial union, a participation in the divine life. As St. Josemaría often said: "It is worthwhile!"[140]

The mind does not find it difficult to understand that this eternal recompense is appropriate. It made sense to Origen:

> [It is proper that] every being which shares in the eternal nature itself would exist forevermore ... for it expresses the eternity of the divine loving-kindness.... Would it

---

[140] *Vale la pena!*

not seem godless to assume that a spirit capable of relating to God should suffer destruction in its substance?[141]

Trust in the reward is not a matter of choice. The Almighty wants it. Writing to the Hebrews, St. Paul states: "Whoever would draw near to God must believe that he exists and that he rewards those who seek him" (Heb. 11:6).

A Fitting Reward

The remuneration the shielded Lover prepares for those who persevere in searching for Him is to see Him face-to-face: The ordinary path for millions of persons is to walk in faith, hope, and love. Eternal Light and eternal Love are the recompense for those who have walked both in hope and in shadow.

On the other hand, there is a suspicion, if not some belief, that sicknesses are related to sinful behavior and may constitute a warning from the Lord. Some see a reproach from God in the high incidence of AIDS, attributing it to sodomy, which is a grievous offense and a mockery of the plan of the Creator, who oriented sexual powers to procreation. Psychiatric practice reveals that in many cases, abortion results in a lifetime of remorse and psychological anguish. Every act of sodomy, fornication, abortion, and destruction of nature is visited with physical or mental retribution, which manifests the discreet ways of the Creator. It seems that He hides His hand not only when He rewards good actions but also when He punishes evil.

But if every single forbidden act were accompanied by a dreadful disease, God would no longer be concealed. Good works

---

[141] Cited in Joseph Cardinal Ratzinger, *God Is Near Us*, 132.

would lose their merit, for many people would behave well out of fear, not out of love. But the Almighty is a wise and gentle Judge, who knows how to deal with His free creatures whom He has put on probation. It is up to Him to decide which acts to punish, when, and in what manner.

Aguiló pointed out that

on many occasions we ask ourselves why God remains silent, why He does not act immediately as it may seem to us logical to do. We wish that He would show Himself more cogently, that He would act in a more forceful manner, that He would defeat evil once and for all, and create a better world.

But when human beings try to organize the world according to their judgment, the result is a world made worse. They ought to exert influence to improve the world without forgetting the Lord of history. As Benedict XVI so beautifully pointed out, "We might suffer on account of God's patience, but we all need God's patience. The world is saved by the Crucified, not by the crucifiers. The world is redeemed by the patience of God and destroyed by the impatience of men."[142]

AIDS, HIV, and the Silent Avenger

The inconspicuous God is simultaneously a Lover, a Creator, an Examiner, a Judge, a merciful Father, an amused Player, a silent Witness, a wise Ruler, the Rewarder of all good deeds, and the just Avenger of every bad action. The way He rights the wrongs

---

[142] Aguiló, *La Llamada de Dios*, 167.

without overwhelming with fear is remarkable. A case in point is the plague of AIDS. Jutta Burgaff states:

> We cannot make any absolute connection between the greatness of one's sufferings and the greatness of one's sins: "As he passed by, he saw a man blind from birth. And his disciples asked him, 'Rabbi, who sinned, this man or his parents, that he was blind?'" Jesus answered, 'It was not that this man sinned, or his parents, but that the works of God might be made manifest in him' (John 9:1–3).
>
> All the bad things in this world are in some way the consequence of sin. There is always a dimension of pun‑ishment — not for a specific person but for all men. It has been this way ever since the fall of our first parents. The Bible tells it all (cf. Gen. 3:6–19). It is also true that the AIDS epidemic came about because of the sins of specific persons who, in a mysterious way, add to the sorrows of the rest of the world.
>
> The Maker punishes to heal and straighten: "But when we are judged by the Lord, we are chastened so that we may not be condemned along with the world" (1 Cor. 11:32). This serious illness is a call, just like all other setbacks that we suffer in life. It is important for us to learn to listen to the divine calls.[143]

It would be wrong to tell a person with HIV or AIDS that his illness was in consequence of his transgressions, for judgment belongs to God alone. But viewed globally, behind the sad occurrences is a subtle admonition coming from the unseen Lord,

---

[143] Jutta Burgraff, *Letters to David* (Manila: Sinag-tala, 2003), 49.

like the blowing of a whistle, not from a policeman but from the most loving and concerned of fathers.

Scott Hahn tells something striking in this regard:

> The pleasure in sinning is the first punishment for sin. This comes as a surprise to most people. We think of divine punishment as a vendetta by which God gets even with sinners. But the worst temporal punishments God allows are the attachments that arise from sins freely chosen. Drunks, for example, don't start off as drunks. The drunkenness is the punishment for the sin of immoderate drinking.... If we do not repent, then we will feel within our souls the weight of this illicit good, bringing us downward, further away from God.... When disaster strikes, the sinner usually thinks that God is finally waking up and beginning to punish him. But this is not wrath; it is divine mercy, saving the sinner from a worst everlasting fate. What we then see as punishments, as wrath, are really the flashes of light that God sends to illustrate a soul darkened by concupiscence and sin.[144]

From the perspective of faith, the ways of the unseen Father, including retribution, are mysterious but always just, merciful, and infinitely wise.

The Sweetest and the Most Bitter Words

When the time comes for the end of the test, the sweetest words we could imagine hearing from Christ would be: "Come, O blessed of my Father, inherit the kingdom prepared for you

---

[144] Scott Hahn, *Lord, Have Mercy!*, 87–88.

from the foundation of the world" (Matt. 25:34). Christ's invitation "Come" is always one of transcendent love: "Come to me, all who labor and are heavy laden, and I will give you rest" (Matt. 11:28).

In contrast, the bitterest words would be: "Depart from me!" (Matt. 35:41) or: "I tell you, I do not know where you come from; depart from me, all you workers of iniquity" (Luke 13:27).

From this perspective, the sweetest and the bitterest words coming from Jesus' lips are "come" and "depart," because man's greatest call is to come to search, to find, adore, and be united with God forever. To depart from Him is the exact opposite.

The Unavoidable

On earth, God leaves man free, much like a teacher who gives a test to his students and leaves them to do their work. He sees some pupils diligently taking the test, others less involved, still others wasting time, and some just fooling around. He lets them be, but at the end of the testing period, he says: "It is time! Come and submit your papers!"

When the time comes for human beings to "submit their papers," God will become uncompromising, in marked contrast with the gentle, quiet Proctor of our lives. Now He will call for an account of our stewardship. This is the encounter to which we will be summoned. The covering veil will be removed quickly and unexpectedly in the case of sudden death.

11

God and the Scientists

When I look at thy heavens, the work of thy
fingers, the moon and the stars which thou hast
established; what is man that thou art mindful of him,
and the son of man that thou dost care for him?

—Psalm 8:3–4

Knowledge puffs up, but love builds up.

—1 Corinthians 8:1

Now comes a particularly important matter—namely, the relationship between the unseen Maker and empirical scientists. The subject is significant, for modern man has come to value much—and not infrequently to overvalue—the findings of empirical scientists. Today, science and technology have often replaced philosophy and religion.

What we have seen so far is that God hides from human beings, including, of course, experimental scientists. God hides from everybody because He wants everybody to take the great and universal earthly test of faith.

Why God Hides

Ronald Knox wrote:

God hides Himself in His creation; or rather, He reveals Himself in His creation, but in such a way that it is possible not to see Him. He does not deceive us, but He allows us to deceive ourselves.... It only needs a little obstinacy of mind to look God's creation in the face and steadily refuse to go back beyond it or argue upwards from it. Man has the dreadful power of refusing to think. And for the most part when people do that, they are only rationalizing what is really an attitude of the will; their will is enslaved by God's creatures and therefore their mind will not raise itself above God's creatures.[145]

Benedict XVI related creation with reason: "Creation is born of the Logos and indelibly bears the mark of the creative Reason which orders and directs it."[146]

In a speech delivered before President Clinton in the East Room of the White House, on the occasion of the unveiling of the Human Genome Project, Dr. Francis Collins, who was an atheist before he became a believer, said:

It's a happy day for the world. It is humbling for me, and awe-inspiring, to realize that we have caught the first glimpse of our own instruction book, previously known only to God.... Many will be puzzled by these sentiments, assuming that a rigorous scientist could not also be a serious believer in a transcendent God.... Belief in God can be an entirely rational choice, and ... the principles

---

[145] Knox, A Retreat for Lay People, 77.
[146] Benedict XVI, Verbum Domini, no. 8.

of faith are, in fact, complementary with the principles of science.[147]

He added,

If God is outside of nature, then He is outside of space and time.... God could, in the moment of creation of the universe, also know every detail of the future. That could include the formation of the stars, planets, and galaxies, all of the chemistry, physics, geology, and biology that led to the formation of life on earth, and the evolution of humans, right to the moment of your reading this book — and beyond. In that context evolution could appear to us as driven by chance, but from God's perspective the outcome would be entirely specified. Thus, God could be completely and intimately involved in the creation of all species, while from our perspective, limited as it is by the tyranny of linear time, this would appear a random and undirected process.[148]

Yet there are empirical scientists who, perhaps because of their deep immersion in the physical world, have become as if imprisoned in it. They find it hard to go beyond the physical realm to enter the metaphysical domain. They offer no satisfactory answers to the most important questions concerning human existence.

A noted Spanish author, Prof. Juan Luis Lorda, puts it well:

With eyes that are too materialistic, it is difficult to appreciate beauty and it is more difficult still to see God....

[147] Collins, *The Language of God*, 3.
[148] Ibid., 205.

The positive sciences have a proper way of seeing things which consists in breaking them to pieces. They try to know how things are made up or constructed—what are their material parts and components and how they are structured. Thus, there is a tendency to think that each thing is simply the sum total of its material parts, to reduce the whole to its parts, and this can give a *materialistic vision* to those who dedicate themselves to cultivate such sciences.

This vision is useful in many ways, but in others it becomes an obstacle. It makes it hard to grasp the vision of the whole; it is an impediment to the realization that often, the whole is not reducible to its parts, and besides, with such outlook, one does not know what to do with things that cannot be broken up. For instance, the beauty of a landscape cannot be divided into parts, nor can it be said that the beauty of a poem is the sum total of its components.[149]

Albert Einstein's comment that a man of science is a poor philosopher[150] appears to be related to this ontological reductionism. In fact, reality is infinitely richer than the physical world, and should not be reduced to it.

Although there are many distinguished scientists who believe in God, there are also many who abhor metaphysics and religion. This seems to be the case with the late biologist Richard Dawkins,

---

[149] Juan Luis Lorda, *Moral: El arte de vivir* (Madrid: Ediciones Palabra, 2006), 204.

[150] Albert Einstein, *Out of My Later Years* (New York: Philosophical Library, 1950), 59.

who, in his book *A Devil's Chaplain*,[151] frontally attacks religion. He focuses on negative aspects, such as the squandering of the natural world rather than on its harmony, order, and beauty. This is just one more instance of there being enough light for those who want to believe, and enough darkness for those who do not.

In his work *The Blind Watchmaker*, Dawkins claims that nature is like a watch, and the watchmaker is a blind, impersonal maker. His reference to Darwin's natural selection reveals a worldview where there is neither room nor need for God. Similarly, empirical scientist Jacques Monod stated that "man knows at last that he is alone in the universe's unfeeling immensity, out of which he emerged only by chance."[152]

Such a statement stands in sharp contrast to the remark of Professor Artigas at the end of an analysis of teleology in nature:

> Scientific progress does not contradict God's plan; on the contrary, the more we know how created causes behave, the more we should admire the greatness of a God who communicates to creatures the capacity to collaborate with Him to achieve goals that represent both the fulfillment of God's plans and the perfection of the created agents.[153]

God's existence and agency are not "scientifically demonstrated." Following the methods of empirical science, Peter Schuster, the president of the Austrian Academy of Sciences, affirms:

---

[151] Richard Dawkins, *El capellan del diablo* (Barcelona: Editorial Gedisa, 2005).

[152] Jacques Monod, *Chance and Necessity* (New York: Alfred A. Knopf, 1971), 180.

[153] Mariano Artigas, *The Mind of the Universe* (Philadelphia: Templeton Foundation Press, 2000), 146.

"The natural scientist at present is making not a single observation that could be explained compellingly only by the interference of a supernatural being."[154] And yet scientific research affords the greatest number of opportunities to take the metaphysical steps leading to God as the uncaused Cause and the ultimate end of everything in the observable world.

There are different positions regarding God's presence in the physical world.

One of them identifies the physical world with God. Such is the position of Fred Hoyle, a Cambridge astronomer who stated that "God was by definition the Universe and the Universe God."[155] This is a pantheistic position that cannot be reconciled with sound philosophical principles, for an imperfect world cannot be identified with Him.

Another position views nature as utterly distant from the architect of the world. This is a deist view that contradicts the notion of God as a caring Father.

Between these two poles is another position that conforms to the experience of reality and is free from philosophical objections. This view, while upholding God's transcendence and distinction from nature, recognizes the Creator's immanence and agency in the world.

Some people refer to nature as Mother Nature, as if nature were a kind of goddess and as if to avoid any reference to God. But God is the Creator of the universe, who is present in beings more than they are present to themselves. Referring to this, a

[154] Quoted in *Creation and Evolution*, 58.

[155] Fred Hoyle and Chandra Wickramasinghe, *Evolution from Space: A Theory of Cosmic Creationism* (New York: Simon and Schuster, 1981), 143.

contemporary author, Joséf Zycinski, offers the following observation: "The gap between a scientific and a religious vision of
the world is, to a great extent, the result of the fact that in clas-
sically understood natural theology, the thesis of His immanence
in nature did not obtain sufficient attention."[156] The same author
mentions specific manifestations of the immanent action of the
Almighty in physical processes:

> Among many physical forms of manifestations of the
> divine immanence, we have to notice in particular: (1)
> the very existence of the laws of nature in a world which
> would exist as a lawless disorder; (2) the emergence of new
> attributes that constituted the domain of pure possibilities
> in the earlier stages of the cosmic evolution.[157]

These considerations point to the fact that evolution, far
from denying the Lord, requires an Intelligent Maker, an Organizer who has *programmed* it. Prof. Artigas adds the following
insight to this view:

> This suggests that we should think of a God who is not
> a mere architect, working to order preexisting material
> from outside. Divine action is conceived as the cause of
> the very nature of the material components of our world,
> including their interaction, patterning, and successive
> steps of self-organization.... This insight leads us to the
> idea of purpose, which plays a central role as a bridge that

[156] Jósef Zycinski, *Three Cultures* (Arizona: Pachart Publishing
House, 1990), 60.

[157] Jósef Zycinski, *The Interplay between Scientific and Theological
Worldviews*, ed. Niels H. Gregersen and Ulf Gurman (Geneva:
Labor et Fides, 1999), 3–19.

joins science to metaphysics and religion.... The acceptance of divine purpose makes it possible to understand
how necessity, chance, and purpose can be combined to
bring about our world. Indeed, if naturalist explanations
were to be considered ultimate, we would be forced to
attribute to blind forces a subtlety and foresight they
cannot possess.... Indeed, the combination of lawfulness
and chance seems most fitting for the development of a
historical course that follows the laws of nature and is also
directed by God's design.

One of the more relevant innovations in the current
scientific worldview is that nature is seen as the source
and result of a huge process of self-organization with a
historical character.[158]

Along the same lines, Zycinski notes:

The acceptance of a rational principle of the dynamism
of nature makes possible the evasion of many former
controversies connected with the dilemma: "either necessity or purpose," and enables rational explanations of the
ultimate causes of biological evolution.[159]

The fact that in the physical world there are fixed laws that
empirical scientists can detect and translate into mathemati-
cal formulae does not exclude the reality of a purpose intended
by physical actions—a purpose, a teleology, that is bound to
remit the observer into theology, that is, the discovery of the

---

[158] Artigas, *The Mind of the Universe*, 327–328.
[159] Zycinski, *Three Cultures*, 44.

anonymous Maker. This amounts to taking an ontological leap unto the transcendental world while remaining firmly fixed in reality.

The above, and many other considerations, lead to the realization that the Almighty does, indeed, intervene in nature, and always in wise, skillful, discreet ways, for He manages to remain silent and withdrawn throughout all His actions. To that effect, in every instance, He "leaves the door open" for whoever might want to get out of the believing room and join the salon of the agnostics and atheists.

The Lord guarantees freedom and emerges as impressive with His creative, directive, and propelling power as He does with his ability to "hide His hand." The perception of the latter skill leads us to inquire for the reason God might have for "covering His Hand," with the hope of gaining an insight into His way of acting. It is a query this book attempts to answer.

There might be some statistical basis for Albert Einstein's assertion that scientists make poor philosophers. It would seem as if the mental habit of viewing reality from a purely positivistic standpoint would make some scientists uncomfortable with nonquantitative realities. In making that remark, Einstein might have wanted to say that, generally speaking, empirical scientists are not used to asking questions about the ultimate causes regarding reality, which is the fundamental task of a philosopher. Einstein's well-known statement could also show an excessively solid, self-built mental wall between two realms: physics and metaphysics.

Although the empirical scientist, as such, is not expected to ask metaphysical or religious questions, it is easy to realize that every human being is called to be a philosopher, *a lover of wisdom,* and thus, ultimately, to inquire about the Almighty. He might at times speak strictly as an experimental scientist. But if what is implied here is that a person cannot be a philosopher and an empirical scientist at the same time, such an affirmation would be utterly wrong.

In fact, physical experiments lead, in a very natural way, to philosophical inquiries. Thus, John M. Templeton and Robert L. Herrmann pointed out how science leads to questions that fall beyond its scope:

> What is the meaning of a universe in which the principal assembly of fundamental particles eventually manifests the potential for organization into complex forms that are conscious and self-conscious, and thereby transcend that matter from which they were derived? Science thus paradoxically seems to lead us, in our search for intelligibility and meaning, beyond the realm of science.[160]

"It is overstepping a boundary," says Cardinal Schönborn, "when the natural scientist denies, for instance his subjectivity (which makes it possible for him to pursue science in the first place) along with the concomitant metaphysical reality."[161]

Ultimately, it comes to this: even though empirical science in itself does not prove God's existence and agency, its findings invite the scientists to ask themselves ultimate questions that belong to higher levels, such as metaphysics and religion.

On January 15, 2007, *Time* magazine published the article "God vs. Science," in which Francis Collins took the side of God, and Richard Dawkins the side of science. When *Time* asked

---

[160] John M. Templeton and Robert L. Herrmann, *The God Who Would be Known* (San Francisco: Harper and Row, 1989), 38.
[161] Quoted in *Creation and Evolution*, 128.

Dawkins whether God is a delusion, he answered, "The question of whether there exists a supernatural creator, a God, is one of the most important that we have to answer. I think it is a scientific question. My answer is no."

By asserting that the existence of a supernatural creator is a scientific question, Dawkins shows his conviction that the only science to be recognized and to be trusted is empirical science. According to him, since the Maker is not the object of our senses, God is not identifiable. Dawkins, and all who think like him, are in dire need of moving beyond physics and entering into metaphysics, where they could find the Almighty.

Time then asked Francis Collins if he believed that science is compatible with Christian faith. He replied:

> Yes, God's existence is either true or not. But calling it a scientific question implies that the tools of science can provide the answer. From my perspective, God cannot be completely contained within nature, and therefore God's existence is outside of science's ability to really weigh in.

With this declaration, Collins does not preclude that God can be known through other ways, such as metaphysics and faith, and makes it clear that

> one can be a rigorous scientist and at the same time a serious believer in a transcendent God. My research gave me the opportunity of glimpsing God. When one sees for the first time the 3.1 billions of letters in the "book of instructions" (the human genome) that transmit all kinds of information as well as the mysteries concerning humanity, it is not possible to look at one page after another without

feeling perplexed, full of expectation; and it is easy to recognize a superior mind—God. Science is compatible with transcendence.

In answer to the negative view of nature brought up by Richard Dawkins, we can say that since our world is no longer Paradise but rather a testing ground, we should expect from it neither too much, such as a perfect world, nor too little, such as a world full of evil. There is a certain duality in our planet that could be considered as hinted by these words of Isaiah: "Then the LORD will create over the whole site of Mount Zion and over her assemblies a cloud by day, and smoke and the shining of a flaming fire by night" (4:5).

With what relish St. Josemaría Escrivá quoted this passage. For him, aside from the obvious reference to signs established by Yahweh to guide the Chosen People through the wilderness, these words of Isaiah applied to Yahweh making things of very different kind: some are attractive, such as fire with its splendor, and others repulsive, such as smoke; for in nature, not all is beautiful and appealing to the eyes, not all is pleasant and understandable to our limited minds. Our world is under the stigma of sin. Our world, marked with the *cosmic consequences of sin*, is certainly no longer Paradise.

Since, from all eternity, God knew about the eventual fall of Adam and Eve due to their misuse of freedom, He created the universe neither as a garden of delights nor a Gehenna of misery, but as a testing ground, an exile where good and evil, pleasure and pain coexist.

The imperfections, the cruelty, and the shortcomings of nature should not surprise or scandalize anyone; they are the *smoke* that reminds man of the Fall. Like smoke, they are repulsive but not morally evil. The countless wonderful marvels of the world make up the *fire* that reminds man of the lost Paradise.

The Path to Wisdom

The path to wisdom, which is concerned with ultimate realities, ascends from physics to metaphysics, which, in turn, leads to the highest point, religion, with the discovery of God. God is eager to be discovered and glad when man succeeds. He helps man at every step along the way, gently, so as not to deprive him of freedom and merit, yet with effective firmness. It is the wisdom that Pope Benedict XVI displayed at the inauguration of his pontificate when he said: "We are not some casual and meaningless product of evolution. Each of us is the result of a thought of God. Each of us is willed, each of us is loved, each of us is necessary."[162]

It must be said here that the empirical path is valid, with its concern for the immediate reasons of phenomena. It is the proper way for experimental research. The supremacy of the intellect is sometimes taken as an unquestionable premise. This rationalist attitude sets human reason on a pedestal so that it becomes a false god. One could set reason above all things, refusing to surrender to the Supreme Being, who could be discovered just by common sense. But, says Dr. Francis Collins, "science is not the only way of knowing. The spiritual worldview provides another way of finding truth. Scientists who deny this would be well advised to consider the limits of their own tools."[163]

---

[162] Speech delivered during the inauguration of Pope Benedict XVI, April 24, 2005.

[163] Collins, *The Language of God*, 229.

Why God Hides

A person's unwillingness to surrender before the Lord comes from a lack of desire to acknowledge the existence of a Creator from whom he has received his being, to whom he owes respect, worship, gratitude, love, and obedience. Whatever the causes, the fact is that some experimental scientists—in sharp contrast with other equally competent colleagues who are firm theists—have declared themselves agnostics or atheists.

The Convert and the Pope on Science

Dr. Francis Collins, describing his path to faith, wrote:

> It also became clear to me that science, despite its unquestionable powers in unraveling the mysteries of the natural world, would get me no further in resolving the question of God. If God exists, He must be outside the natural world, and therefore the tools of science are not the right ones to learn about Him.[164]

Benedict XVI warned that science, "in its joy over the greatness of its discoveries, tends to confiscate dimensions of our reason that we still need. Its findings lead to questions that reach beyond its methodological principles and cannot be answered within science itself."[165]

Creation

Man can best perceive the Maker's existence and agency through creation. St. Paul asserted that "ever since the creation of the

---

[164] Ibid., 30.
[165] Quoted in *Creation and Evolution*, 163.

world his invisible nature, namely, his eternal power and deity, has been clearly perceived in the things that have been made" (Rom. 1:20). Echoing this trust in human powers, the Church declared in unambiguous terms that "if anyone says that the one true God, our Creator and Lord, cannot be known with certainty with the natural light of reason through the things that are created, *anathema sit*."[166]

For Dr. Francis Collins, "The Big Bang cries out for a divine explanation. It forces the conclusion that nature had a defined beginning. I cannot see how nature could have created itself. Only a supernatural force that is outside of space and time could have done that."[167] The same author affirms: "The existence of the Big Bang begs the question of what came before that and who or what was responsible."[168]

An empirical scientist, with his mind-set, might say: "This reality can be explained by molecular mechanisms, genetic pathways, and natural selection." This prosaic explanation refers only to the immediate cause, but not to the First Cause, who placed in nature those mechanisms, pathways, and selective drives.

In summary, the two theories about the origin of the universe are the view that God created the world out of nothing (*ex nihilo*) and the view that the universe is self-sufficient and infinite.

Artigas observes:

The real novelty in our times is that a position has been formulated that claims to be based on scientific advances

---

[166] First Vatican Council, *Dei Filius*, chap. 4, canon 2-1. The Church has traditionally used the phrase *anathema sit* (let him be anathema) to issue doctrinal definitions.

[167] Collins, *The Language of God*, 67.

[168] Ibid., 66.

in cosmology and asserts that the universe had a beginning in time but is nonetheless completely independent of any divine act of creation. This means a kind of creation without a creator.[169]

Science alone cannot prove the existence of divine creation. . . . The arguments that can lead us to admit the existence of a divine creation are rather metaphysical and religious.[170]

To talk about creation without a creator, as some empirical scientists do, is to engage in absurdity, because to create is to produce something out of nothing. The universe must first exist before change can happen.

Two contrary theories are advanced. One sees the universe as created by God. The other claims that the universe had a beginning in time, but God had nothing to do with it. But since nothing can come out of nothing, there must be an original reality from which the other beings came. The theory of the "self-creation" of the universe is inconsistent, untenable, and contradictory.

Every creature, the entire universe actually, carries a placard with an inscription: *I do not have in myself the full and ultimate explanation of my being! There is a beginning, there is Another! There is a perfect and supreme spiritual Being! There is God!*

When the world is viewed with an open mind free from materialistic biases, nature appears as a splendid interplay between matter and spirit, like the one presented by Prof. Artigas:

The flow between the spiritual and material world really exists. When we contemplate the natural dynamism, successive deployments and integration produce an immense

---

[169] Artigas, *The Mind of the Universe*, 112.
[170] Ibid., 112–113.

variety of systems and processes that make possible the appearance of the human being. In virtue of our rationality and freedom, we possess a personal character that implies a special participation in the nature of God. We are God's collaborators. God has created a world in becoming, destined to reach more and more evolved goals, and has created human beings as created co-creators who are able to know God's plans and to collaborate with God in a spirit of love and responsibility.[171]

This view assigns man the role of *created co-creators*, secondary causes who contribute to making the world a better and more congenial habitat for human beings — in line with the command received in Paradise: "The LORD God took the man and put him in the garden of Eden to till it and keep it" (Gen. 2:15). It is aligned with the statement of Étienne Gilson: "We must recall what the Christian universe really is: a sum total of creatures owing their existence to an act of love."[172] And it is likewise in line with Cardinal Schönborn's statement: "To believe in creation means to understand, in faith, the world of becoming revealed by science as a meaningful world that comes from a creative mind.[173]

Evolution

Evolution is another area in which God seems hidden from experimental scientists. Since Charles Darwin, theories on evolution

---

[171] Artigas, *The Mind of the Universe*, 339–340.
[172] Gilson, *The Spirit of Mediaeval Philosophy*, 273.
[173] Quoted in *Creation and Evolution*, foreword.

of the species have been mistaken as proofs of the absence of a creator. As a result, a false dichotomy has emerged between creation and evolution.

There is no conflict between creation and evolution from a theological standpoint, provided that it is held that the human soul is created by the Creator in every human conception. Unfortunately, the prestige that experimental sciences presently enjoy is being used to advance pseudoscientific theories with conclusions that fall outside empirical science. Some evolutionists have tried to show that God's providence and action can be replaced by mutation and natural selection.

God is an infinite spirit who transcends time and space and who does not have to act in this way or another. It is a mistake to think that a divine plan means a sequence of events of such a nature that we could recognize the necessary links between them. If this were the case, there could not be contingency involved.

If chance is understood as an accidental coincidence of causes, divine providence is compatible with chance. This is, of course, viewing reality from a human perspective. For God who knows everything, nothing happens by chance.

Even if the evolutionary process that has brought about the existence of humans includes a multitude of contingent events, the existence of a plan by the veiled Creator is compatible with it. In fact, there is no chance if there is no finality, and finality implies intelligence. Seeing that there are countless signs of purpose in nature, we can conclude that there is intelligent activity at the source.

In his interview with Peter Seewald, Cardinal Ratzinger stated: "The Christian picture of the world is this, that the world in its details is the product of a long process of evolution, but at the most profound level it comes from the *Logos*. Thus, it carries rationality within itself."[174]

Evil

Many are "scandalized" by the observation of physical evil in nature and think that it is not compatible with a divine plan for the world. This is nothing else but a consequence of the limitations of the created cosmos. The Maker is not bound to make a perfect world. God acts with infinite freedom. He made creatures that fascinate as well as horrify. Some are attractive, others repulsive, some impressive, others funny.

Part of the evil in the world is due to moral evil, sin, the result of misuse and abuse of freedom. God permits evil, stated St. Thomas Aquinas, for the sake of a greater good. Physical evil is also not contrary to divine goodness.

A great number of scientists see nature as a multiform manifestation of the power and wisdom of God. Among them is Dr. Francis Collins, who states:

> How deeply satisfying is the digital elegance of DNA! How aesthetically appealing and artistically sublime are the components of living things from the ribosome that translates RNA into protein, to the metamorphosis of the caterpillar into the butterfly, to the fabulous plumage of the peacock attracting his mate! Evolution, as a mechanism, can be and must be true. But that says nothing about the nature of its author. For those who

---

[174] *God and the World: A Conversation with Peter Seewald*, trans. Henry Taylor (San Francisco: Ignatius Press, 2002), 139.

believe in God, there are reasons now to be more in awe, not less.[175]

This is an accurate appraisal, for nature is the effect of God's agency.

Order in Nature

It is possible that the Maker will allow random physical interactions in the world. Artigas explains it here:

> That God rules the world does not mean that nature behaves in a completely ordered way, according to our own criteria. Therefore, it cannot be argued that the existence of random evolutionary events and the patchwork character of evolutionary adaptations are incompatible with the existence of a divine plan. On the contrary, the existence of many contingent events fits well with a God who respects the mode of being and acting of his creatures because He himself has planned and wanted them. The new discoveries about chaos and complexity may help us understand that a highly sophisticated organization can result from very simple causes that include randomness.[176]

Everything in creation is controlled by the Lord. He Himself said, "Even the hairs of your head are all numbered," and the apostles asked: "What sort of man is this, that even winds and sea obey him?" (Matt. 10:30; 8:27). But lest pure and rigid

---

[175] Collins, *The Language of God*, 107.
[176] Artigas, *The Mind of the Universe*, 151.

directionality be taken as proof of His existence, the anonymous Maker has allowed portions of the evolutionary process to develop at random. Thus, His actuation in nature does not appear overwhelmingly obvious and is one more instance of God's hiding His hand.

John Polkinghorne studied chaos theory in relation to the action of God, and concluded:

> God's action will always be hidden. It will be contained within the cloudy unpredictabilities of what is going on. It may be discernible by faith, but it will not be exhibitable by experiment. Although much of the physical world is cloudy and unpredictable, there are also clockwork and predictable parts of what is going on. This regularity will be to the believer signs of divine faithfulness. The picture given is of an open future in which both human and divine agency play parts in its accomplishment. Petitionary prayer can be exercised with scientific integrity.[177]

This summary of empirical research placed against faith states in the first conclusion that "God's action will always be hidden." Such a categorical assertion prompts the question "Why is this so?" The answer to this most intriguing question is precisely the object of our consideration.

In the second conclusion is a worldview in which directionality and unpredictability coexist. If everything were chaotic, not even empirical science would exist. On the other hand, if an

---

[177] John Polkinghorne, "Chaos Theory and Divine Action" in *Religion and Science, History, Method, Dialogue*, ed. W. Mark Richardson and Wesley J. Wildman (New York: Routledge, 1996), 248–250.

evident directionality exists in all phases of the natural processes, God would cease to be the unseen Planner He wants to be.

The third conclusion has to do with God's willingness to take man as a "created co-creator," who, using the mind the Creator granted him, can modify present forms and provoke the appearance of new ones. The command given in Paradise to till the earth implies more than pure maintenance of existing creatures; it implies using the mind to improve the world and to produce new creatures.

The last conclusion points out that there is nothing in experimental science that makes prayer useless, for the Maker retains full control of all that happens. He is omniscient and almighty, and from the scientific point of view, the contemporary worldview underlines contingency and unpredictability. The order in the physical world is contingent and results from specific circumstances. Gone are the days when the world was the only one possible. In the present view of nature there is room for new and unpredictable realities. The world is not a closed and rigid system, but one in which there is organization, directionality, and complexity of activities. At the same time, there is a Maker who continues being involved in everything. In light of this flexibility and contingency, it is reasonable to ask God for favors, even concerning natural realities, such as cures for sickness.

Albert Einstein had been quoted as saying: "Man finds God behind every door that science manages to open." and "Religion without science would be blind, and science without religion would limp."[178]

---

[178] See Aguiló, *Es razonable ser creyente*, 41, 51.

God and the Scientists

The Narrow Escape

In their book *El Planeta Privilegiado* (*The Privileged Planet*), Guillermo Gonzalez, an astronomer, and Jay W. Richards of the Acton Institute show that in the Milky Way, Earth enjoys the privileges of the presence of water, of harmony between Earth and the moon, and of the gravitational pull from Jupiter and Saturn, which protects Earth from meteors and asteroids. Their explanation:

> The fact that our atmosphere is clear, that our moon is just the right size and distance from the earth, and that its gravity stabilizes the earth's rotation; that our position in our galaxy is just so, that our sun is its precise mass and composition: all of these factors (and many more), are not only necessary for earth's habitability; they also have been surprisingly crucial for scientists to measure and make discoveries about the universe.[179]

In the course of history, countless persons have come to realize that it is thanks to the position of Earth in the galaxy that life is possible. If our planet were only a bit closer to the sun, our weather would be unbearably hot, and if it were a bit farther from it, we would freeze to death. This has become known among scientists as the "narrow escape." From the perspective of faith, the "narrow escape" indicates the amazing wisdom displayed by the Creator, who, through His divine agency, has ordered all things.

Patterns in Nature

A scientific law is established on the basis of the repeated occurrence of a certain phenomenon. This is why scientists are

---

[179] See de Torre, *The Historical Genesis of Modern Science*, 42.

ever on the lookout for patterns in nature. To mention a simple example, the repeated observation of objects falling toward the center of the earth gave rise to the law of gravitation and the computing of its acceleration.

There are innumerable patterns in nature, and this leads to the question of their origin. If the world were mere chaos, there would be no patterns at all, but since this is not the case, the question arises: What mind has organized these systems? Artigas says:

> Science presupposes that patterns exist, and they can be explained on the grounds of other natural patterns.... Nature is rational insofar as it has been formed according to rational principles and because it provides the basis for the existence of rational beings.[180]

The existence of patterns in nature is the basis of St. Thomas Aquinas's fifth way of demonstrating the existence of God.

Speaking from the perspective of empirical scientists and showing full understanding of their viewpoint, Artigas mentions several instances that show that there is rationality in the way nature is structured and acts. The many patterns that exist in nature are proofs of such rationality. Artigas brings up another indication that the physical world implies intelligence:

> Nature is rational because it includes a huge series of processes that are integrated in a very sophisticated way. One may wonder, indeed, how it is possible to reach so many varied results with so few elements.... Thus, three sub-atomic particles [protons, neutrons, and electrons] are the basic constituents of ordinary matter; 92 atoms

---

[180] Ibid., 124.

are the components of a great variety of natural systems; four nucleotides are the elements of the highly sophisticated genetic information; some twenty amino acids are the components of proteins. Subtlety in methods and sophistication in results are the rule in nature.[181]

Then he states:

Science alone cannot prove the existence of divine creation. Indeed, from a scientific point of view, we can always suppose that some state of the universe, elementary as it may be, was the result of other preceding states. But the arguments that can lead us to admit the existence of a divine creation are metaphysical and religious.... Empirical science presupposes the existence of nature and studies the production of new entities and processes from some preexistent grounding. If a divine agency exists, it cannot be studied by the methods of empirical science.... The ultimate ontological foundation of the universe is a metaphysical problem that must be dealt with using philosophical arguments and cannot be settled through merely physical arguments.[182]

He quotes William Carroll: "No theory in the natural sciences can contradict the doctrine of creation, since what creation accounts for is not a process at all but a metaphysical dependence in the order of being."[183]

---

[181] Ibid.

[182] Ibid., 114–115.

[183] William E. Carroll, "Big Bang Cosmology, Quantum Tunneling from Nothing, and Creation," *Laval Théologique et Philosophique* 44 (1988): 68, 70.

Why God Hides

Indeed, the unseen Maker is not expected to be discovered by experiential science in the way that elements such as uranium or plutonium were discovered.

Finality in Nature

One of the most obvious indications of the existence of an intelligent Creator is based on the observation that finality is present in the physical world, since to act for a purpose requires rationality. The latter is the case of the "intelligence" exhibited by a bird building a nest or by a tree growing from roots that pick out nutrients from the earth. In both instances there is teleology (acting for a purpose), and yet both creatures lack the spiritual faculty of intelligence. The subject of such rationality cannot be a purely material entity. They are examples of a "programmed reality" that points to a supremely intelligent, albeit secluded, programmer.

The main problem scientists face is how to cover the gap between physics and metaphysics. Finality is one of the bridges capable of reaching both sides.

Artigas explains it here:

> Natural teleology can be a road to God because it shows that natural tendencies produce highly rational results providing the basis for the existence of truly rational beings. Natural teleology is also compatible with the existence of contingent elements and partial drawbacks. Of course, arguments based on natural teleology cannot provide a detailed knowledge of God's plans.... As our world is full of stabilized organization and has been formed through a huge process of self-organization, it is

completely legitimate to use teleological categories to study the world and to talk about it.[184]

Finality in nature is one of the evident features of the physical world, and yet there are in our time many anti-teleological assertions due to the inability of a number of empirical scientists to "climb the metaphysical ladder."[185]

Miracles and Science

The April 9, 2007, *Newsweek* article "The God Debate" covered the contention between Rick Warren, a Christian pastor and well-known author, and Sam Harris, a professed atheist. Harris told Warren:

> You could prove to the satisfaction of every scientist that intercessory prayer works if you set up a simple experiment. Get a billion Christians to pray for a single amputee. Get them to pray that God redraws that missing limb. This happens to salamanders every day, presumably without prayer; this is within the power of God. I find it interesting that people of faith only tend to pray for conditions that are self-limiting.

There is no need for such an experiment, for it has happened that a man's leg was restored in a miraculous way: the well-documented case of the miracle of Calanda in Aragon, Spain. Vittorio Messori, a renowned Italian convert from atheism wrote a book about it.[186]

---

[184] Ibid., 145.

[185] Ibid., 127.

[186] See Jose Manuel Vidal, "El Milagro de Calanda Resucita," *Epoca*, November 16, 1998.

The point is that Christians do not make experiments of this sort, nor of the kind where a man dead for many decades may be brought back to life. The reason is that believers do not want to put God to a test. Since they understand the game they are playing, they ask only for favors that will not require an overpowering manifestation of the unseen Almighty, who wants to remain a hidden donor.

Sam Harris claimed that a magician could do the miracles Jesus performed. But the miracles recorded in the Gospel's accounts — the raising of Lazarus, who had been dead for four days, the raising of the son of the widow of Naim, the raising of the daughter of Jairus, the return of sight to Bartimeus, the walking on water, the calming of the water on His command, the changing of water into wine, the multiplication of bread and fish to feed thousands of people, and so on — were more than acts of a performer. In the Gospels, there are twenty passages referring to Jesus' working miracles and curing the sick. The enthusiasm of the people originated from witnessing His wonders. Since His enemies could not deny these miracles, they alleged that He worked them by the power of Beelzebub, "the prince of the demons" (Matt. 12:24). The way that miracles are recounted in the Gospels is very different from the style proper to legends, as can be seen by comparing the Gospels with the apocryphal accounts. The evangelists are much more factual and restrained.

The historicity of these miracles is further supported by the existence of non-Christian sources, such as the Jewish historian Flavius Josephus, who, in his book *Jewish Antiquities* written in Greek circa A.D. 93, refers to miracles worked by Jesus.

Those who adopt Mr. Harris's position are asking for a kind of evidence that does not belong to historical science.

God and the Scientists

The Predicament of Agnostics and Atheists

The most fundamental drive of intellectual activity is to explain reality, beginning with wonder, striving for wisdom, and ending up discovering the hidden God. He is the ultimate explanation of all that is perceived, the Alpha and the Omega of everything. But He is purposefully veiled, the object not of the senses but of the mind. It is a matter of climbing from the physical to the metaphysical level. The sterling achievement of metaphysics is to discover the Supreme Being, Truth, Goodness, and Beauty. It gives great joy, for it satisfies the deepest craving of the human intellect and will. In this theistic light, a coherent and convincing worldview is acquired. The Maker and Lord hiding behind every event, even the most ordinary, can be revealed. As Artigas puts it:

> In the light of scientific progress, nature can be seen as a multiform manifestation of the power and wisdom of God. All human beings, also considered in their natural dimensions, represent a most sophisticated kind of natural organization that can easily become a pointer toward the divine. Any kind of event can be considered an opportunity to find a divine meaning in our lives; we should not identify the divine with extraordinary circumstances. God's involvement with creation is so deep that He can be found in the most ordinary circumstances of any human life.[187]

Another author adds, "We must come to terms with the fact ... that we live in a world in which almost everything which

---

[187] Artigas, *The Mind of the Universe*, 331–332.

is very important is left essentially unexplained.... Ultimately everything is left unexplained."[188]

It is a very sad and awful situation to resist the light that comes from the Lord. The psalmist referred to this when he said, "The rebellious dwell in a parched land" (Ps. 68:6).

Referring to the well-known position of Richard Dawkins, which sees evolution as leading to atheism, Dr. Francis Collins has this to say: "The major and inescapable flaw of Dawkins' claim that science demands atheism is that it goes beyond the evidence. If God is outside nature, then science can neither prove nor disprove His existence."[189]

God and the Thinkers

Many great thinkers of all time have come to the discovery of the latent God, even though throughout the centuries, the Lord has also not been recognized by individuals who devoted time to explain reality.

Philosophy (the love of wisdom) should lead to Him who is Wisdom itself. But many modern philosophers, taking a subjectivist path, have lost touch with reality, the sure link with God. Stanley Jaki states:

True realism is about the continued existence of things and, above all, the continued consistent existence of the totality of things which is the universe. Such realism may seem to be plain common sense. In fact, it is a rare and most precious commodity. A quick look at the cacophony

[188] Karl R. Popper, *The Self and Its Brain* (New York: Springer, 1977), 554–555.
[189] Collins, *The Language of God*, 165.

of modern philosophies will make that commodity appear an almost gratuitous gift, a grace of sorts.... Clearly, realism which is fully rational must be part and parcel of a revelation that has for its starting point the self-revelation of God as He Who Is, or existence itself, and culminates in a Divine Logos incarnate in human flesh.

Jaki continues with this anecdote:

In an International Conference on ecology and religion, a prominent Hindu emphatically challenged me on my claim about the central importance of the idea of creation out of nothing as the basis for any religion worthy of rational respect. According to him, it was a fatal pretension to say that there is an essential difference between existent and non-existent, the real and the nothing. I urged him to do business with his bank or with his grocer on this basis.[190]

The foregoing has tried to show that God hides from empirical scientists as well as from speculative thinkers who do not want to take the leap from physics to metaphysics, and to the Maker Himself, despite countless promptings from Him. There is no meeting ground because He does not want to be discovered through physical methods, which are proper to the experimental sciences, nor by unnecessary disclosures. The psalmist puts in the mouth of the wicked this question: "How can God know? Is there knowledge in the Most High?" (Ps. 73:11). There is certainly knowledge in the unseen Lord, but God will not reveal Himself to those who, for whatever reason, do not wish to see Him.

---

[190] Stanley Jaki, *The Only Chaos*, 14.

12

God and Man, Friends

By his Revelation, the invisible God, from the fullness of his love, addresses men as his friends and moves among them, in order to invite them into his own company.

—*Dei Verbum*, no. 2

Consequently the Word Who from the beginning is with God and is God, reveals God himself in the dialogue of love between the divine persons, and invites us to share in that love.

— Benedict XVI, *Verbum Domini*, no. 6.

On July 29, 2009, the Holy Father referred to a wrist fracture he suffered some days before: "Unfortunately, my guardian angel did not stop my fall, and surely did so following orders from above. Perhaps, the Lord wanted to teach me to be more patient and humble, and give me more time for prayer and meditation. It was not a coincidence."[191] This comment is an excellent model of how to interpret events.

[191] Rome Reports, "Benedict XVI: With this injury, the Lord wants to teach me to be patient," YouTube video, 0:17, July 29, 2009, https://www.youtube.com/watch?v=UATIK34T76g.

Why God Hides

The veiled Father loves us immensely. He helps men meet the challenges of life, small or not so small, speaking through the varied events of our earthly journey. We might be hardheaded and deaf to what He is saying, so it is important to ask the Holy Spirit's advice on how to deal with the silent Father and His Son, Jesus Christ.

To Seek Him First

To make a conscious effort to *penetrate the veil* is hard. For that task, the help of the Holy Spirit, who moves men to seek, find, and love God and to do His Will, is indispensable. It is He who brings us to the Father, and what is needed is docility to His action.

The point is not to allow earthly things to prevent penetration of the *world above*, even if the materials of our conversation with God are earthly things. We have the assurance of our Lord, who said: "You will seek me and find me; when you seek me with all your heart, I will be found by you" (Jer. 29:13–14). In our search, it will help to realize that He is always waiting for us.

Bishop Alvaro del Portillo was moved by what he heard during a trip to Africa, to the effect that when one climbs a mountain, the effort is made easier when a loved one is waiting at the peak. From the Sacred Text, we know that He is waiting for us in His glorious state. "The end of history," affirms Vatican II, "has already reached us, and the renewal of the world is already decided irrevocably and in some real way is already anticipated in this world."[192]

---

[192] Second Vatican Council, Dogmatic Constitution on the Church *Lumen Gentium* (November 21, 1964), no. 48.

God and Man, Friends

Friends across the Border

In the writings of some spiritual authors we find expressions such as these: "On that occasion, the Lord gave me prayer" or "That afternoon I found it hard to enter into prayer." St. Teresa of Avila would speak of such things as "*tener oración*" (to have prayer) or "*entrar en oracion*" (to enter into prayer).

Man is expected to cooperate with the Lord in *piercing the veil* and *crossing the border*, to exercise faith in all the activities of ordinary life. This is what it means, as St. Josemaría was fond of saying, to be "contemplatives in the midst of the world."

The *Catechism of the Catholic Church* describes prayer as "a gift of grace and a determined response on our part." That response requires our effort. Prayer is a battle "against ourselves and against the wiles of the tempter who does all he can to turn us away from prayer, away from union with God" (CCC 2725).

The Gospels say that on several occasions people were looking for Jesus. St. John tells us: "When the people saw that Jesus was not there, nor his disciples, they themselves got into the boats and went to Capernaum, seeking Jesus" (John 6:24). We too are to seek the Lord, even though at times it appears that He is absent because He is as a Lover, eager to discover in us the slightest sign of interest. Didn't he say, "Behold, I stand at the door and knock?" (Rev. 3:20). This is man's destiny and sweet duty: to look for our Friend and Lover, who wants to be sought, found, and loved.

St. Mary Faustina Kowalska said:

I was very sad due to the fact that Jesus suffers on account of chosen souls, and Jesus told me: "Their love is lukewarm; My heart cannot stand it; these souls oblige Me to reject them. Some do not trust My goodness and they never want to experience the sweet intimacy in their heart, but they seek Me somewhere out there, far away, and they do not find Me. This lack of confidence in My goodness is what hurts Me most. If My death has not convinced them of My love, what will convince them?"[193]

St. Teresa of Avila said of our relationship with the Friend and veiled Lover:

When He allowed that all would see Him manifestly, and was telling them clearly Who He was, they did not treat Him well. In fact, only a few believed in Him. Therefore, He shows us great mercy when His majesty wants that we understand that it is He who is in the Blessed Sacrament. But He only wants that we see Him openly and only wants to communicate His greatness and His treasures to those who desire it very much, for these are the true friends. Thus, whoever does not come to welcome Him as a friend, to this one He will not manifest Himself.[194]

Dealings with the Veiled Friend

One of the Church's most beautiful liturgical hymns, "*Adoro Te Devote*," was composed by St. Thomas Aquinas in the thirteenth century. It begins with: "I adore you devoutly, hidden Deity." The Angelic Doctor, much impressed by the reality that the great

---

[193] Quoted in Jose Pedro Manglano, *Junio* (Madrid: Ediciones Co-bel, 2008), 10–11.

[194] Jesús Martí Ballester, *Teresa de Jesús nos habla hoy: Suma antológica* (Madrid: San Pablo, 1994), 13.

Love of our lives is concealed, expressed in this hymn his great longing for the sight of the Almighty.

God is out of sight not only to agnostics and atheists but to a multitude of believing but distracted humans. Those who, by the grace of God, have discovered the unseen Father and the "cloud of witnesses" (Heb. 12:1) have a greater obligation to keep their look heavenward, to be contemplatives. Contemplation should not be the spiritual luxury of a few mystically inclined people, for it is a universal call. Contemplation consists in taking the Lord seriously and in conducting a lively friendship with Him.

Dr. Francisco Ponz described the way he witnessed St. Josemaría live the presence of God: "He always reflected a positive vision, good humor, and a bit of supernatural salt that was never burdensome — proper of someone who was in the habitual presence of God and wanted to bring others to Him."[195]

Friendship with God

After establishing a friendship with the hidden Lover, it is important to maintain a constant rapport. St. Bonaventure desired this constancy in his famous prayer: "May You alone be ever my hope, my entire assurance, my riches, my delight, my pleasure, my joy, my rest, my tranquility, my refreshment, my refuge, my help, my wisdom, my portion, my possession and my treasure."[196]

St. Josemaría, in *Friends of God*, offers this suggestion on how to relate with the Almighty:

---

[195] Francisco Ponz Piedrafita, *Mi Encuentro con el Fundador del Opus Dei* (Pamplona: EUNSA, 2000), 45.

[196] Cf. Charles Belmonte and James Socias, *Handbook of Prayers* (Manila: Sinag-tala, 2005), 212.

Rest assured that it is not difficult to convert work into
a prayerful dialogue. As soon as you offer it up and then
set to work, God is already listening and giving encouragement. We acquire the style of contemplative souls,
in the midst of our daily work! Because we become certain that He is watching us while He asks us to conquer
ourselves anew: a little sacrifice here, a smile there for
someone who bothers us, beginning the least pleasant but
most urgent job first, carefulness in little details of order,
perseverance in the fulfilment of our duty when it would
be so easy to abandon it, not leaving for tomorrow what
should be finished today: and all this, to please him, our
Father God![197]

The awareness of the silent Father is important in the life of
a Christian and leads to a contemplative attitude. It is in this
light that we understand the statement in *The Way:* "An hour of
study, for a modern apostle, is an hour of prayer." St. Catherine
of Siena, a Doctor of the Church, stressed God's presence at all
times. She sensed from her youth that the meaning of life could
be found only "connecting with the other world," the supernatural, the divine. For her, the everyday world of family and friends,
cares, and excitement, suffering and ceaseless struggles was, in
the end, transient and unreal.

Over and over, she told those who came to her for spiritual
truths that they must enter the presence of the "First Truth." This
is done, she said, "by selfless loving, praying, doing good works,
keeping the commandments, by remaining pure and by offering

[197] St. Josemaría Escrivá, *Friends of God* (Manila: Sinag-tala, 2000),
no. 67.

up work, joy, and suffering to God."[198] Catherine was gifted with a sense of the importance of connecting with the other world, with the appreciation of the separation of the barrier between "here" and "there," as well as with the existence and immense worth of that other world. Centuries later, St. Josemaría will call it "holding a double citizenship." Said he: "Your Christian vocation requires you to be in God, and at the same time, to be concerned with the things of the earth, using them objectively, just as they are, to give them back to Him."[199]

Seeing God

The highest degree of intimacy with God is achieved by the souls in Heaven, who, through the beatific union, participate in the divine life. The Lord is manifest to them—*Deus Patens*—and their vision is perfect and effortless.

As for us in this life, Jesus tells us: "Blessed are the pure in heart, for they shall see God" (Matt. 5:8). The Almighty gives to those who have pure hearts the light necessary to perceive supernatural realities. George Chevrot wrote:

Not everyone can see Him, because a light veil clouds our view. This veil is often woven from morally imperfect dispositions. The knowledge of God, in fact, is not the conclusion of a reasoning process. If a creator who is at the same time our master exists, another question arises: that of our duties toward Him. He has a right not only to the assent of our intelligence; He imposes Himself on our

---

[198] Quoted in *Inside the Vatican* (April 2002), 42.
[199] *Furrow*, no. 295; cf. nos. 290–322.

liberty. And that is why a more or less dense fog comes between God and men, hiding Him from them.... One must love the truth more than oneself, not balking at the consequences it would entail, but striving to face it. If one is "completely pure, completely without pride," then one can see God.

For Christians, the problem of God poses itself in very different ways. From the fact of his union with Jesus Christ, the Christian is not seeking God, nor is he worried about His existence: this question seems frivolous to him. He lives in His presence, he "sees God." He reaches Him by faith, which Pascal defined as "God perceptible to the heart" and which one should not compare with an emotion or a feeling of exaltation.[200]

The withdrawn Examiner tests with great trials the souls of those who love Him. This is the dark night of the soul experienced by St. John of the Cross and St. Teresa of Calcutta. This way of purification seems to thicken the veil for these souls so that they would grow even closer to Him. To them it is a source of consolation to consider that Jesus too had His dark night of the soul on the Cross when He cried out: "My God, my God, why hast thou forsaken me?" (Matt. 27:46).

In the ascetical struggle, the great goal of the spiritual life is to regain, to the extent possible, the familiarity with Yahweh that Adam and Eve lost in Paradise. If these dealings with the veiled Interlocutor were to appear to be boring, there is some mistake. Cardinal Ratzinger wrote: "In our dealings with God, there is

---

[200] Georges Chevrot, *The Eight Beatitudes* (Manila: Sinag-tala, 1998), 165–167.

no boredom. There could, perhaps be such in some practices of piety or some pious readings, but never in an authentic relationship with God."[201]

There are circumstances that could help much in communicating with the Father and the other persons of His Family. They facilitate awareness of being part — *through Him, with Him, and in Him* — of a single Body, the Church. Dr. Francisco Ponz cites a personal experience: "I recall keeping watch at night in advanced military posts in Balaguer — I felt very vividly God's presence."[202] It is easy to picture the young military officer fulfilling his duty, simultaneously a contemplative immersed in the Almighty.

The Great Audience

The Great Audience is there even when it seems as if nobody cares. Bishop Javier Echevarría put it this way: "Let us not desert from prayer on account of the false idea that we are not heard."[203]

We are like theater actors who do not see the audience because they sit in the dark. Such a perception notwithstanding, the Lord, his angels and saints are our audience. For as St. Paul wrote: "We have become a spectacle to the world, to angels and to men" (1 Cor. 4:9). We ought to communicate with this most distinguished audience all the time. To succeed in this endeavor even in a limited fashion amounts to a degree of contemplation; which is the mission both of those called to live in the world and

---

[201] Cardinal Joseph Ratzinger, *La Sal de la Tierra: Una conversación con Peter Seewald* (Madrid: Ediciones Palabra, 1997), 13.

[202] Ponz Piedrafita, *Mi encuentro con el Fundador del Opus Dei*, 28.

[203] Echevarría, *Getsemani*, 194.

of those called to withdraw from it. This contemplation enlarges the outlook toward the cloud of witnesses, which covers the expanse of the other world.

This discovery of the hidden Lover should be made not only in extraordinary circumstances, but also while going about the most prosaic activities. The Founder of Opus Dei said on occasion, "This detail [or this window or this door] is finished with a little love of God." In 1962, he said at a family gathering, "God passes constantly at your side! He is not escaping from you; you do not see Him simply because you do not seek Him. Open well your eyes to look at the Lord."[204]

Connect!

How is it possible for someone who has spent much time meditating daily eventually to abandon our Lord? It must be that he did not truly connect with the hidden Lord. He may have used the precious time for prayer in petty monologues, speaking to himself.

St. Josemaría tells of a true connection when he wrote:

Today once again I prayed full of confidence. This was my petition: "Lord, may neither our past wretchedness which has been forgiven us, nor the possibility of future wretchedness, cause us any disquiet. May we abandon ourselves into your merciful hands. May we bring before you our desires for sanctity and apostolate which are hidden like embers under the ashes of an apparent coldness."

---

[204] Javier Echevarría, *Memoria del Beato Josemaría Escrivá* (Madrid: Ediciones Rialp, 2000), 271.

"Lord, I know you are listening to us." You should say this to Him, too.[205]

Love Back the Veiled Lover

The shielded Lord is not a cold, indifferent onlooker of our struggles on earth; He attracts us to Himself with refinement and power, *suaviter et fortiter*, while ever keeping His condition of a veiled Suitor.

To explain this, St. Augustine quoted Sacred Scripture:

> Nobody can come to Me, if he is not attracted by the Father. Let it not be that you think that you are attracted against your will; the soul is also attracted by Love.... It seems to me little to say that we are attracted freely; we are to say that we are even attracted with pleasure. What does it mean to be attracted with pleasure? "Let the Lord be your delight; and He will give you what your heart asks of you." There is an appetite of the soul to which this heavenly bread tastes as very sweet.... Could we not say that man feels attracted by Christ, if we know that the delight of man is truth, justice, life everlasting, and Christ is all these?[206]

Sacred Scripture describes God's love in this way: "My beloved is like a gazelle, or a young stag. Behold, there he stands behind our wall, gazing in at the windows, looking through the lattice" (Song of Sol. 2:9). The Lord attracts, nay, seduces us, not by imposing His Love, but by giving us an appetite, a longing,

---

[205] Escrivá, *The Forge*, no. 426.
[206] Augustine, *Ex Tractatibus*, tract 26, 4–6, see CCC 36 and 261.

an absolute need for Him. Only He, infinite Truth, can satiate our intellect; only He, infinite Goodness, can satisfy our will. And therefore, as the great Augustine said: "Lord, our hearts are restless until they rest in You."[207]

Show God to Everyone

To seek the veiled God, to find Him through faith, to hope in Him, and to love, adore, and serve Him is a great service to mankind and constitutes the essence of all apostolic endeavors. St. Josemaría reiterates: "Christ is not a figure of the past. He is not a memory lost in history. He lives!"[208] As St. Paul says, "Jesus Christ is the same yesterday and today and forever" (Heb. 13:8).

As its invisible Head, He leads the one, holy, catholic, and apostolic Church that He founded. The scope of His wish is expressed in this declaration: "I do not pray for these only, but also for those who believe in me through their word" (John 17:20). It is a magnificent thing to be included in that pronoun "those," and even more, to be able to include many others in the expanding apostolic wave.

Jesus said to the apostle Thomas: "Blessed are those who have not seen and yet believe" (John 20:29). It is encouraging that these words apply to all who believe and become witnesses of the Risen Christ.

Many are eager to see Jesus, but they will have to see Him through us. Dom Chautard explains that

one of the most formidable obstacles to the conversion of a soul is that God is hidden. But God in His goodness

---

[207] Augustine, *Confessions*, bk. 1, chap. 1.
[208] *The Way*, no. 584.

reveals Himself, in a certain manner, through His saints, and through fervent souls. In this way, the supernatural filters through, and becomes visible to the faithful, who can apprehend something of the mystery of God.[209]

Finding God in the Ordinary

As a lover of nature, a good physician, and a man of God, Cardinal Herranz wrote:

Be quiet, say nothing. Learn, while walking silently, to listen to Him. For so long a time He has been talking to you and you did not listen to Him!

Today, at least today, in this immense solitude, listen to the Other. Many are the years He has been following you, walking at your side, trying to dialogue with you; and you did not let Him.

Alone, you leave Him alone. He wants to be your Way, your Truth, and your Life. And you do not let Him!

Be silent, listen. Start by allowing Him to speak to you and to take a look at the messy hullabaloo of your soul and impose silence. Afterwards, let your first words be only these: "forgive me!"[210]

The silent Almighty ought to be discovered behind all the realities of nature. It is easy in the cases of the marvelous complexity of the human brain, the beauty and fragrance of a rose, the elegance of a swan, the vigor of a lion, the capricious coloring of

---

[209] Dom J. B. Chautard, *The Soul of the Apostolate* (Manila: Sinagtala, 1985), 119–120.
[210] Herranz, *Atajos del silencio*, 67.

the feathers of a parrot, the splendor of a sunset, or the silence of a green valley. All of these are reminiscent of the original Paradise that the Good Lord wanted us to enjoy.

Admittedly, it is not easy to recognize God behind calamities, sickness, death, and other puzzling realities proper to our earthly exile. But we can take a cue from St. Paul, who, moved by the Holy Spirit, said:

> I consider that the sufferings of this present time are not worth comparing with the glory that is to be revealed to us. For the creation waits with eager longing for the revealing of the sons of God; for the creation was subjected to futility, not of its own will but by the will of him who subjected it in hope; because the creation itself will be set free from its bondage to decay and obtain the glorious liberty of the children of God. We know that the whole creation has been groaning in travail together until now (Rom. 8:18–22).

Only Christianity gives an acceptable answer for those disconcerting realities and considers them as opportunities to co-redeem with Jesus Christ in this world, which is experiencing the groaning proper to the period of expectation until there are "new heavens and a new earth" (2 Pet. 3:13).

The Invisible through the Visible

St. Josemaría suggested an excellent way to reach the invisible world. In a homily he gave in 1967 on the campus of the University of Navarre, he said: "We discover the invisible God in the most visible and material things. There is no other way. Either we learn to find our Lord in ordinary, everyday life, or else we shall never find Him."[211] This great saint of the twentieth century, whom Pope John Paul II called "the saint of the ordinary," looked at material things not as mere screens covering spiritual realities but as *vehicles* to reach them and reach God Himself. This is why he called objects used to keep the presence of God "alarm clocks"—that is, objects that awaken us to the supernatural world concealed to our eyes of flesh, but clear to our eyes of faith.

Each one will have to invent his own "human devices" to live in the presence of the Examiner and of the "cloud of witnesses." Pope John Paul II had the habit of writing on the upper right corner of every piece of paper he worked on some words or code—such as the acronym JMJ, in order to remember Jesus, Mary, and Joseph—to help him give a supernatural character to his work.

We Should Not Demand Signs

Prof. Artigas explains the interplay between the Almighty's action and man's:

> As intelligent and responsible creatures, we should employ our capacities to figure out what we should do. It is left to our free responsibility to recognize our role in God's plan, and to venture toward its implementation with a sense of ethical responsibility. Nobody can replace us. There is an essential openness in nature, in human affairs, and in the construction of the future.

[211] *Conversations with Monsignor Escrivá de Balaguer*, no. 114.

We should always be ready to understand that God's plans might not coincide with our own. Nevertheless, we should also expect that if we really desire to collaborate with God's plans, God will let us know them. Even though our knowledge of God and of God's plans is incomplete, it can provide the necessary basis for our responsible decisions in such a way that we may discover the meaning of our lives and may understand in every particular case what we should do.[212]

Asking for signs is to require the Creator to manifest Himself before we take Him seriously; and while waiting, to go about in a confused and sluggish manner, without giving importance to Him.

St. Augustine says that we should not pretend to understand His ways, for He is infinite while our mind is limited. He states that "if you understand Him, then He is not God."[213]

The piercing of the veil through faith must always be on His terms. We may "pierce the veil" at any time through an act of faith, but St. Josemaría and other spiritual authors discourage people from being "miracle minded."[214] Our Lord Himself exclaimed: "This generation is an evil generation; it seeks a sign, but no sign shall be given to it except the sign of Jonah" (Luke 11:29).

Extraordinary events and spiritual favors do give a boost to the spiritual life, but they also place the burden of responsibility of giving an account to God for them. If granted, they are to be received with gratitude, but they should not be asked for.

[212] Artigas, *The Mind of the Universe*, 331.
[213] Augustine, *Sermo* 52, 16.
[214] See *The Way*, no. 583.

God and Man, Friends

We Should Not Ask for Evidence

In our dealings with persons of the supernatural world, we should not ask for the kind of evidence that natural sciences demand. In the latter, we require proofs that are perceived by our senses. To want the same physical evidence regarding the existence of persons of the transcendental world, however, would be a violation of a fundamental rule of the divine game. It would be comparable to asking a teacher for answers during an exam.

The very fact that we ask for physical proof indicates that we are not sure of their existence. Faith excludes doubt. Asking for perceptible proofs would be tempting God, for it would amount to asking for extraordinary aids from Him, or even the "answer" itself, which, in the ordinary course of events, He would not give us. On the other hand, He does often grant clues, many and excellent, but not the answer, which is Himself.

In the Gospels, Our Lord appears as a beggar of Faith, Who is ever eager to be believed and recognized. Thus, for instance, Jesus told the unbelieving Jews:

> If I am not doing the works of my Father, then do not believe me; but if I do them, even though you do not believe me, believe the works, that you may know and understand that the Father is in me and I am in the Father (John 10:37–38).

On the road to Emmaus, Cleopas and his companion experienced the presence of Jesus Christ, albeit in a somewhat veiled way, and they pleaded with Him, saying, "Stay with us" (Luke 24:29).

Presently, He is for us the *latens Deitas*, the latent Deity; but for all eternity, He will be the *patens Deitas*, the manifested Divinity.

Why God Hides

We Should Not Test the Lord

"The LORD spoke to Ahaz, 'Ask a sign of the LORD your God; let it be deep as Sheol or high as heaven.' But Ahaz said, 'I will not ask, and I will not put the LORD to the test'" (Isa. 7:10–12). Confronted with the reality of a concealed God, we might be tempted to request a sign that He is real. If this temptation comes, the appropriate reaction would be to say, like Ahaz: "I will not put the Lord to the test!"

Physical evidence eliminates the need for faith, which is what human beings are tested about. Thus, Jesus provided physical evidence of His miracles, but not about Himself as God.

Many other texts of Sacred Scripture forbid tempting Yahweh. Moses, after summoning the people of Israel to lay before them the Ten Commandments, told them: "You shall not put the LORD your God to the test, as you tested him at Massah" (Deut. 6:16). The psalmist tells us: "They tested him again and again, and provoked the Holy One of Israel" (Ps. 78:41). Christ Himself, aware of the Pharisees, said, "Why put me to the test, you hypocrites?" (Matt. 22:18). And to Satan He said: "It is written, 'You shall not tempt the Lord your God'" (Matt. 4:7).

Cardinal Ratzinger says this:

> The Bible describes this rebellion against God as follows: They put the Lord to the proof by saying, "Is the Lord among us or not?" (Exod. 17:7). The issue, then, is the one we have encountered: God has to submit to experiment. He is "tested," just as products are tested. He must submit to the conditions that we say are necessary if we are to reach certainty.... The arrogance that would make God an object and impose our laboratory conditions upon him is incapable of finding him. For it already implies that

we deny God as God by placing ourselves above him, by discarding the whole dimension of love, of interior listening; by no longer acknowledging as real anything but what we can experimentally test and grasp.[215]

The book of Wisdom says it clearly, "He is found by those who do not put Him to the test, and manifests himself to those who do not distrust him" (Wisd. 1:2).

Trust during Difficulties

"Lord, have You really forgiven me?" It is not surprising to seek reassurance on such an important matter. In these instances, the temptation is to interpret difficulty or misfortune as signs of God's displeasure. Often God permits suffering for a person's good. Mary and Joseph went through great hardships during the flight to Egypt, but no one can think that these trials were signs of God's displeasure.

Even when we do not understand situations in our lives, we must persevere in searching for the living God. When Jesus was lost in the Temple, Mary and Joseph did not comprehend what was happening. When they found him, "his mother said to him, 'Son, why have you treated us so? Behold, your father and I have been looking for you anxiously.' And he said to them, 'How is it that you sought me? Did you not know that I must be in my Father's house?' And they did not understand the saying which he spoke to them" (Luke 2:48–50). Yet they were wise enough "to understand that they could not understand," as the Founder of Opus Dei was fond of saying.

---

[215] Benedict XVI, *Jesus of Nazareth*, 37.

Why God Hides

Maintain Peace

St. Thérèse of Lisieux's motto was "I shall not get discouraged!" According to her, what offends Jesus and wounds Him to the Heart is want of confidence. Thérèse knew how to concentrate on what she was doing without worrying about the next task. She spoke in a pleasant tone and spread serenity among those she met and lived with. Even her way of moving around the house exuded serenity. She put into practice St. Paul's advice:

> Have no anxiety about anything, but in everything by prayer and supplication with thanksgiving let your requests be made known to God. And the peace of God, which passes all understanding, will keep your hearts and your minds in Christ Jesus. (Phil. 4:6–7)

Thérèse also followed the famous injunction of her mentor St. Teresa of Jesus: "Let nothing disturb you! Let nothing scare you! Patience obtains all things! God alone is enough!"[216]

St. Josemaría shows us the path to obtain interior peace: "The wholehearted acceptance of the Will of God is the sure way of finding joy and peace, and happiness in the Cross. It's then we realize that Christ's yoke is sweet and His burden is light."[217] Christ himself said: "Learn from me; for I am gentle and lowly in heart, and you will find rest for your souls" (Matt. 11:29).

St. Josemaría makes this suggestion:

> Are you suffering some great tribulation? Do you have reverses? Say very slowly, as if savoring the words, this

---

[216] *Nada te turbe; nada te espante; la paciencia todo lo alcanza; solo Dios basta.*

[217] Escrivá, *The Way*, no. 758.

powerful and manly prayer: "May the most just and most lovable Will of God be done, be fulfilled, be praised and eternally exalted above all things. Amen." I assure you that you'll find peace.[218]

Jacques Philippe affirms:

We often torment ourselves too much on account of our decisions.... This desire of knowing what the Almighty wants concealed and our difficulty in enduring uncertainty: we want to be freed from having to decide by ourselves. And yet, the will of the Lord is that we know how to decide about matters, even if we are not absolutely sure that this decision is the best.[219]

Mindfulness of Our Communion with God

The greatest mistake is to think that because the Almighty is not perceived and is silent, He is not there or does not care. In reality, He is the most loving Father the world will ever know.

Baptism is participation in the life of the Trinity. The sanctifying grace from this sacrament is a grafting into God's life. Through grace, we enter into the Lord's world, and we become divinized as adopted children of God. St. Peter even said that we become "partakers of the divine nature" (2 Pet. 1:4). St. Paul tells us, "You are no longer strangers and sojourners, but you are fellow citizens with the saints and members of the household of God" (Eph. 2:19).

---

[218] Ibid., no. 691.
[219] Philippe, *La paz interior*, 70.

Why God Hides

This awareness that we are children of God, partakers of the divine nature, and members of God's household should dispel feelings of loneliness. Even if people were indifferent toward us, the Lord and all in the heavenly company of witnesses are united with us in a sterling bond of love and grace.

In light of this, let us not immerse ourselves in petty things — in an empty, superficial, and animal life. Let the Almighty, Our Lady, and the rest of the supernatural world be in our thoughts. Let us earnestly be mindful of the presence of God, rather than limit ourselves to insubstantial and perhaps inane or immoral concerns.

This Passing Life

Life on earth is transitory. Death marks the lifting of the veil, when the decisive moment has come. We are meant to transcend this world and to reach the next world, which, for the saved, will be permanent, definitive, and immensely better from all points of view. St. Teresa of Jesus said, "O, how little that of here, how much that of there!"[220]

We should not install ourselves in this world, as if it were for keeps. "Here we have no lasting city" (Heb. 13:14). The deaths of relatives, friends, and acquaintances serve as reminders of this sober truth.

Constant Attentiveness to God

Many people spend their lives ignoring the veiled Lover, only to run to Him at the last moment, when sickness and death are at the door.

---

[220] *O cuan poco lo de acá, O cuan mucho lo de allá!*

God and Man, Friends

Alfonso Aguiló wrote:

Many people take God as a mere resort when in difficulty. They ask Him things as if He were a plumber whom they call when a faucet breaks down or a leak appears. But those who are close to God do not act this way. They realize that God is not there only to solve the domestic problems; He is there constantly to illumine their life.[221]

We tend to live as if God were not right here, in our own circumstances. We often postpone taking care of our relationship with Him: "I will take care of my spiritual life after I pass the exams" or "after I get married" or "when the kids are grown up" or "when I retire" or "when I am financially stable." St. Josemaría Escrivá, with characteristic clear strokes of his pen, suggested the remedy:

God is no shadowy or distant being who created us, and then abandoned us; nor is He a master who goes away and does not return. Though we do not perceive Him with our senses, His existence is far truer than any of the realities which we touch and see. God is here with us, really present, living. He sees and hears us; He guides us, and knows our smallest deeds, our most hidden intentions.

We believe, but we live as if God did not exist. For we do not have a thought or a word of Him; for we do not obey Him, nor try to control our passions; for we do not show that we love Him, and we do not atone.

Are we going to live with *a dead faith?*[222]

---

[221] Aguiló, *La Llamada de Dios*, 181.
[222] Escrivá, *Furrow*, no. 658.

Why God Hides

Seeing God's Hand

There is a story of a lady caught in a very bad flood. A boat came to rescue her, but she refused. "No, no. I am praying to God. He will save me!" As the water rose, a second boat came to her rescue, but she replied in the same manner. Finally, when the water was so high that she had climbed onto the roof, a helicopter arrived, but she shouted, "No, no, God will save me!" When she died and complained to the Lord, He told her: "But I sent you two boats and a helicopter!"

Let us not be so blind in recognizing God's hand in the events of life.

13

Jesus Christ, the Ultimate Revelation

*Without having seen him you love him; though
you do not now see him you believe in him and
rejoice with unutterable and exalted joy.*

—1 Peter 1:8

Christians should be eager to lift this world from its pettiness to true greatness, but this task can be accomplished only through the mediation of Jesus Christ. St. Paul calls us "to re-establish all things in Christ" (see Eph. 1:10), and St. Josemaría says, "We want Christ to reign!"[223]

"I am the way, and the truth, and the life," Jesus tells us. "No one comes to the Father, but by me" (John 14:6). Right there lies the answer to man's deepest, most vital longing in his life—to see God! The bridge over the divide is no other than Jesus Christ, the God-Man. Through St. Catherine of Siena, God said:

I told you that I have made a bridge of the Word, my only-begotten Son, and such is the truth I want you to realize,

---

[223] *Regnare Christum volumus!*

my children, that by Adam's sinful disobedience, the road was so broken up that no one could reach everlasting life.

I want you to look at the bridge of my only-begotten Son and notice its greatness. Look! It stretches from heaven to earth, joining the earth of your humanity with the greatness of the Godhead.[224]

The future Benedict XVI wrote:

Life shared with God, eternal life within temporal life, is possible because of God living with us: Christ is God being here with us. In him God has time for us; he is God's time for us and thus at the same time the opening of time into eternity. God is no longer the distant and indeterminate God to whom no bridge will reach; he is the God at hand; the Body of the Son is the bridge for our souls.... God is no longer merely a God up there, but God surrounds us from above, from below, and from within. He is all in all.[225]

The greatest manifestation of the Almighty to mankind occurred when the Word was made flesh in the womb of Mary, the maiden of Nazareth. This is how God facilitated man's discovery and love for Him through His splendid and sacred Humanity. When the fullness of time arrived, the light came in the person of Jesus Christ.

Pope Benedict affirmed:

True, no one has ever seen God as He is. And yet God is not totally invisible to us. He does not remain completely

---

[224] St. Catherine of Siena, *The Dialogue*, nos. 21, 22.
[225] Ratzinger, *God Is Near Us*, 144.

inaccessible.... God has made Himself visible. In Jesus we are able to see the Father (1 John 4:9).[226]

Yet Jesus' light is not like the overwhelming one of heaven. Man's earthly pilgrimage takes place among shadows since it requires faith and free cooperation with grace.

The Restraint of Jesus Christ

Jesus was born without display in Bethlehem and lived silently in Nazareth. Even His greatest miracle, His Resurrection, was not worked with fanfare. He quietly left His tomb empty. Nobody saw Him rising from the dead. He appeared many times afterward to different people. All was done according to His characteristic discretion.

With the exception of the episode in the Temple in Jerusalem when He was twelve, when He amazed the teachers of Israel with His knowledge and wisdom, Jesus spent thirty years of His life without revealing His divinity. In the eyes of His contemporaries, He was just the son of Joseph, the working man. At the wedding in Cana and at the request of His mother, Mary, He performed the first of His signs by changing water into wine.

From that moment, His hidden life was over, and His public life began. Throughout the next three years, He showed much restraint, even while he worked great wonders. Many times, He told witnesses not to tell anyone about what they had seen. In great part, this was due to His wish not to be mistaken for a new political or religious leader, like Moses, Joshua, or Judas

---

[226] Benedict XVI, *Deus Caritas Est*, no. 17.

Maccabeus. At that time, the expectation among the Jews was for a Messiah to liberate them from the Roman yoke.

But an important reason for Christ's restraint was His desire to remain concealed. Ronald Knox states:

> In the Incarnation, God is half revealed and half concealed; that is the point. He revealed Himself, but not in a way to startle or cow the imagination.... Why did He do that? Partly, of course, in order to exercise our faith. Conviction should not force itself upon the mind. There should be a loophole, once again, by which doubt could creep in, if men were resolved to doubt.[227]

He did none of His miracles to entertain or for display, or set up an exhibition. That is why, when Herod, out of curiosity, asked Jesus to work a miracle, he got neither his request nor a reply. Rather, "the healing miracles that Christ performs in the Gospel demonstrate that God has drawn near to humanity. With this, Jesus wants to reveal the countenance of the true God, the God who is near, full of mercy for every human being, the God who makes a gift to us of life in abundance, of his own life.[228]

Christ Makes Exceptions

Jesus is the ever-enamored Lover. Like people in love, He makes exceptions to the rules of the game. A good example is the Transfiguration on Mount Tabor. For a few minutes, Peter, John, and James were gifted with an extraordinary proof of Christ's divinity. Jesus prepared them for future trials by

---

[227] Knox, *A Retreat for Lay People*, 83.
[228] Benedict XVI, address delivered on January 27, 2008.

showing Himself in His divinity, talking to Elijah and Moses, both of whom had died many centuries before. In those great moments the disciples hardly needed faith. That experience was not a trial, but an affectionate caress. In those unforgettable moments that made them tremble, they felt taken to a higher order of things. But this was an exception and everything was soon back to normal.

In the Acts of the Apostles, Simon Peter is quoted as saying: "God raised him on the third day and made him manifest; not to all the people but to us who were chosen by God as witnesses" (Acts 10:40–41). Christ often made self-disclosures on a selective basis. The Gospel of St. Luke records one such disclosure to his apostles:

In that same hour he rejoiced in the Holy Spirit and said, "I thank thee, Father, Lord of heaven and earth, that thou hast hidden these things from the wise and understanding and revealed them to babes; yea, Father, for such was thy gracious will. All things have been delivered to me by my Father; and no one knows who the Son is except the Father, or who the Father is except the Son and anyone to whom the Son chooses to reveal him (Luke 10:21–22).

In John's Gospel we hear Jesus say:

"Now is my soul troubled. And what shall I say? 'Father, save me from this hour'? No, for this purpose I have come to this hour. Father, glorify thy name." Then a voice came from heaven, "I have glorified it, and I will glorify it again." The crowd standing by heard it and said that it had thundered. Others said, "An angel has spoken to him." Jesus answered, "This voice has come for your sake, not for mine." (John 12:27–30)

Why God Hides

Astonishing Mercy

Jesus expressed His merciful attitude when He gave the assurance that "there will be more joy in heaven over one sinner who repents than over ninety-nine righteous persons who need no repentance" (Luke 15:7); when He made it clear that He did not want the sinner to die but to be converted from his ways and to live (Ezek. 33:11); and when He said, "I have not come to call the righteous, but sinners" (Matt. 9:13).

Jesus' Parables

The following passage from Matthew's Gospel gives insight into the *rationale* for the Almighty's ways of dealing with man:

> Then the disciples came and said to him, "Why do you speak to them in parables?" And he answered them, "To you it has been given to know the secrets of the kingdom of heaven, but to them it has not been given.... This is why I speak to them in parables, because seeing they do not see, and hearing they do not hear, nor do they understand." (Matt. 13:10–11, 13)

These words fulfill the prophecy of Isaiah which goes: "You shall indeed hear but never understand, and you shall indeed see but never perceive" (Matt. 13:14). He only mentions the immediate reason for parables, so that they will not understand the ultimate purpose He had, which was mercy.

That is, to those who had faith in Him, Jesus spoke plainly, for they could take the responsibility that came with understanding. He refused to speak clearly to listeners who did not heed his message, afraid of the heavy burden on Judgment Day, because "everyone to whom much is given, of him will much be required"

(Luke 12:48). Jesus spoke to the crowd in parables to help those with goodwill, but not add a burden on those who do not believe. "If any man has ears to hear, let him hear" (Mark 4:23).

The Almighty is very careful not to burden the conscience of anyone, for He knows that the one who is well exposed to and receptive of His message has to give an account. He will not manifest Himself to those who are not disposed to receive Him, lest it be taken against them on Judgment Day. To such as these, He spoke only in parables. It is a touching manifestation of His wisdom and mercy.

In St. John's Gospel, our Lord explains this, saying: "I have said this to you in figures; the hour is coming when I shall no longer speak to you in figures but tell you plainly of the Father" (John 16:25).

Delicate and Refined

During His stay on earth, Jesus Christ worked more than enough miracles to prove His divinity. Many times, he exhorted witnesses not to tell anyone about them. He always avoided stepping on man's freedom and responsibility, for with light comes an added duty.

Christ continues to ask everyone the question he put to Simon Peter: "Who do you say that I am?" (Matt. 16:15).

Who am I for you: a myth, a legendary person?

Do you recognize me for who I truly am: your redeemer, your teacher, your light, and your resurrection?

Am I absolutely real to you?

Am I, for you, the same yesterday, now, and forever?

Bibliography

Adam, Karl. *The Son of God*. New York: Scepter, 1992.

Aguiló, Alfonso. *Es la religión Cristiana la verdadera?* Madrid: Ediciones Palabra, 2009.

——. *Es razonable creer?* Madrid: Ediciones Palabra, 2009.

——. *Es razonable ser creyente?* Madrid: Ediciones Palabra, 2004.

——. *La llamada de Dios*. 2nd ed. Madrid: Ediciones Palabra, 2009.

Ahlquist, Dale. "A Happy Little Reflection on Hell." *Catholic Servant* (2011).

Alviar, Joselito Jose. *Escatologia*. Spain: EUNSA, 2004.

Artigas, Mariano. *The Mind of the Universe*. Philadelphia: Templeton Foundation Press, 2000.

Artigas, Mariano, and Daniel Turbon. *Origen del hombre*. Pamplona: EUNSA, 2007.

Aumann, Jordan. *Spiritual Theology*. Manila: UST Faculty of Theology, Manila, 1989.

Bacani, Teodoro. *Manila Standard Today*, December 30, 2004.

Ballester, Jesús Martí. *Teresa de Jesús nos habla hoy: Suma antológica*. Madrid: San Pablo, 1994.

Belmonte, Charles, and James Socias. *Handbook of Prayers*. Manila: Sinag-tala, 2005.

Bocala, Henry. *Arise and Walk*. Manila: Paulines, 2009.

Burgraff, Jutta. *Letters to David*. Manila: Sinag-tala, 2003.

Burke, Cormac. *Conscience and Freedom*, 2nd ed. Manila: Sinag-tala, 1992.

Carrel, Alexis. *The Voyage to Lourdes*. Port Huron, MI: Real-View Books, 2006.

Carty, Charles Mortimer. *Padre Pio: The Stigmatist*. Rockford, IL: TAN Books, 1989.

Catholic Encyclopedia. New York: Robert Appleton Company, 1912.

Chautard, Dom J. B. *The Soul of the Apostolate*. Manila: Sinag-tala, 1985.

Chevrot, Georges. *The Eight Beatitudes*. Manila: Sinag-tala, 1998.

Collins, Francis S. *The Language of God*. New York: Free Press, 2006.

Coverdale, John F. *Uncommon Faith*. Princeton, New York: Scepter, 2002.

Dawkins, Richard. *El capellan del diablo*. Barcelona: Editorial Gedisa, 2005.

De Jesus, Lúcia. *Memorias de Lucia: La vidente de Fatima*. 3rd ed. Madrid: Ediciones "Sol de Fátima," 1980.

De Prada, Andres Vazquez. *The Founder of Opus Dei.* Vol. 1. New York: Scepter, 2001.

————. *The Founder of Opus Dei.* Vol. 2. New York: Scepter, 2003.

De Torre, Joseph M. *Contemporary Philosophical Issues in Historical Perspective.* Manila: University of Asia and the Pacific, 2001.

————. *The Historical Genesis of Modern Science and Its Effects upon Civilization and Culture.* Manila: Gabriel Books, 2010.

Delaney, John. *A Woman Clothed with the Sun: The Lady of the Rosary.* Manila: Sinag-tala, 1988.

Echevarría, Javier. *Getsemani: En Oracion con Jesucristo.* Spain: Planeta, 2005.

————. *Memoria del Beato Josemaría Escrivá.* Madrid: Ediciones Rialp, 2000.

Einstein, Albert. *Ideas and Opinions by Albert Einstein.* New York: Crown, 1954.

————. *Lettres a Maurice Solovine.* Paris: Gauthier-Villars, 1956.

————. *Out of My Later Years.* New York: Philosophical Library, 1950.

————. *The World as I See It.* New York: Covici–Friede, 1934.

Figura, Michael. "Faith as the Beginning of Salvation." *Communio International Catholic Review* 22, no. 3 (Fall 1995).

Frossard, André. *Dios existe, yo me lo encontré.* Madrid: Ediciones Rialp, 2002.

Garrigou-Lagrange, Reginald. *The Three Ages of the Interior Life.* Vol. 2. Rockford, Illinois: TAN Books, 1989.

Gilson, Étienne. *The Spirit of Mediaeval Philosophy*. Notre Dame, IN: University of Notre Dame Press, 1991.

Gleick, James. *Chaos: Making a New Science*. New York: Viking, 1987.

Holston, G. Review *Einstein: The Life and Times*, by Ronald W. Clark. *New York Times Book Review*, September 5, 1971, 20.

Hahn, Scott. *Lord, Have Mercy!* New York: Doubleday, 2003.

Herranz, Cardinal Julián. *Atajos del silencio*. Madrid: Ediciones Rialp, 1995.

Holmes, Oliver W. *The Poet at the Breakfast Table*. Boston: James R. Osgood, 1877.

Horn, Stephan Otto, and Siegfried Weidenhofer, eds. *Creation and Evolution: A Conference with Pope Benedict XVI*. San Francisco: Ignatius Press, 2008.

Hoyle, Fred, and Chandra Wickramasinghe. *Evolution from Space: A Theory of Cosmic Creationism*. New York: Simon and Schuster, 1981.

Izquierdo, Cesar. "Palabra (y Silencio) de Dios." *Scripta Theologica* 41, no. 3 (September–December 2009): 954.

Jaki, Stanley L. *Chance or Reality and Other Essays*. Lanham, MD: University Press of America, 1986.

———. *Cosmos and Creator*. Edinburgh: Scottish Academic Press, 1980.

———. *Science and Creation: From Eternal Cycles to an Oscillating Universe*. Edinburgh: Scottish Academic Press, 1973.

———. *The Absolute Beneath the Relative and Other Essays*. Lanham, MD: University Press of America, 1988.

————. *The Only Chaos and Other Essays*. Lanham, MD: University Press of America, 1990.

————. *The Purpose of It All*. Edinburgh: Scottish Academy Press, 1990.

Juliá, Ernesto. *Josemaría Escrivá: Vivencias y recuerdos*. Madrid: Palabra, 2002.

Knox, Ronald. *A Retreat for Lay People*. Lagos: Criterion Publishers, 2005.

Lack, David. *Evolutionary Theory and Christian Belief*. London: Methuen, 1961.

Leite, P. Fernando. *The Apparitions of Fatima*. 3rd ed. Sec. Nacional do Apostolado.

López, Jesus Ortiz. *Palabra*. Madrid: Ediciones Palabra, Sept. 10, 2010.

Lorda, Juan Luis. *Moral: El arte de vivir*. Madrid: Ediciones Palabra, 2006.

Manglano, Jose Pedro. *Junio*. Madrid: Ediciones Cobel, 2008.

Maritain, Jacques. *The Degrees of Knowledge*. 4th ed. Translated by Gerald Phelan. London: Geoffrey Bles, 1959.

Martinez, Luis M. *True Devotion to the Holy Spirit*. Manchester: Sophia Institute Press, 2000.

Messori, Vittorio. *El gran milagro*. Madrid: Editorial Planeta, 1999.

Monod, Jacques. *Chance and Necessity*. New York: Alfred A. Knopf, 1971.

Muntadas, José María. *El Anhelo de Dios*. Madrid: Folletos Mundo Cristiano, 1993.

Newman, Cardinal John Henry. *Letters to the Duke of Norfolk*. London: Longmans Green, 1885.

———. *Parochial and Plain Sermons*. San Francisco: Ignatius Press, 1987.

———. *The Ventures of Faith*. New York: Scepter, 1981.

Olayzola, Jose Luis. *The Loves of Teresa of Avila*. Manila: Sinag-tala, 1999.

OSV's *Catholic Encyclopedia*. Huntington, IN: Our Sunday Visitor, 1991.

———. *The Teaching of Christ: A Catholic Catechism for Adults*. Huntington, IN: Our Sunday Visitor, 1976.

Philippe, Jacques. *La libertad interior*. Madrid: Ediciones Rialp, 2004.

———. *La paz interior*. Madrid: Ediciones Rialp, 2004.

Polkinghorne, John. "Chaos Theory and Divine Action." In *Religion and Science, History, Method, Dialogue*. Edited by W. Mark Richardson and Wesley J. Wildman. New York and London: Routledge, 1996.

Ponz Piedrafita, Francisco. *Mi Encuentro con el Fundador del Opus Dei*. Pamplona: EUNSA, 2000.

Popper, Karl R. *The Self and Its Brain*. New York and London: Springer, 1977.

Rodríguez, Pedro. *La fe como conocimiento de Dios*. Spain: EUNSA, 1974.

Sargent, Daniel. *The Assignments of Antonio Claret*. New Yok: Declan X. McMullen, 1948.

Bibliography

Scheffczyk, Leo. "Faith and Witness: Confesio and martyrium." *Communio International Catholic Review* 22, no. 3 (Fall 1995).

Schlag, Martin. "Theologie der Freiheit." *Scripta Theologica* 42, no. 2 (2010): 489.

Schmaus, Michael. *Curso de Teología Dogmática*, Part 2, *Dios Creador*. Madrid, 1966.

Templeton, John M., ed. *Evidence of Purpose*. New York: Continuum, 1994.

———— and Robert L. Herrmann. *The God Who Would Be Known*. San Francisco: Harper and Row, 1989.

Trigg, Roger. *Rationality and Science: Can Science Explain Everything?* Oxford: Blackwell, 1993.

Velasco, Martin. "La conversión de Manuel García Morente." *Augustinus* 32, nos. 125–128 (1987): 475–497.

Vidal, Jose Manuel. "El Milagro de Calanda Resucita." *Epoca*, November 16, 1998.

White, Kristin. *A Guide to the Saints*. New York: Ivy Books, 1991.

Zyscinski, Joseph, M. *The Interplay between Scientific and Theological Worldviews*. Edited by Niels H. Gregersen and Ulf Gurman. Geneva: Labor et Fides, 1999.

————. *Three Cultures*. Arizona: Pachart Publishing House, 1990.

Works of Saints

Augustine. *Confessions*. New York: Book-of-the-Month Club, 1996.

———. *Ex Tractatibus.*

———. Proslogion. *Biblioteca de Autores Cristianos.*

Catherine of Siena. *The Dialogue.* London: Kegan Paul, Trench, Trubner, 1907.

Escrivá, Josemaría. *Christ Is Passing By.* Manila: Sinag-tala, 1973.

———. *Conversations with Monsignor Escrivá de Balaguer.* Manila: Sinag-tala, 1985.

———. *The Forge.* Manila: Sinag-tala, 2000.

———. *Friends of God.* Manila: Sinag-tala, 2000.

———. *Furrow.* Manila: Sinag-tala, 2000.

———. *Holy Rosary.* Manila: Sinag-tala, 2000.

———. *The Way.* Manila: Sinag-tala, 1985.

———. *The Way of the Cross.* London and New York: Scepter, 1982.

First Vatican Council. Dogmatic Constitution on the Catholic Faith *Dei Filius.* April 24, 1870.

Gregory Nazianzus. *Orationes Theologicae.*

Gregory the Great. *Homiliae in Evangelia.*

John Damascene. *De Fide Orthodoxa.*

John of the Cross. *The Ascent of Mount Carmel, Book 2.*

Teresa of Avila. *The Autobiography, Soliloquies.* New York: Book-of-the-Month Club, 1995.

———. *The Life of Teresa of Jesus: The Autobiography of St. Teresa of Avila.* New York: Doubleday-Image, 1960.

Bibliography

————. *The Way of Perfection*. New York: Image Books, 1964.

Thomas Aquinas. *Summa Contra Gentiles*.

Church Documents and Works of Popes

Benedict XVI. Encyclical *Deus Caritas Est*. December 25, 2005.

————. *Jesus of Nazareth*. New York: Doubleday, 2007.

————. Encyclical Letter *Porta Fidei*. October 11, 2011.

————. Apostolic Exhortation *Verbum Domini*. September 30, 2010.

Compendium of the Catechism of the Catholic Church. 2005.

Francis. Encyclical Letter *Lumen Fidei*. June 29, 2013.

John Paul II. Encyclical Letter *Fides et Ratio*. September 14, 1998.

————. *Cantad al Señor un cántico nuevo*.

————. *Laudes con el Papa: Las catequesis de Juan Pablo II sobre los salmos y cánticos de Laudes*. Madrid: Biblioteca de Autores Cristianos, 2003.

Ratzinger, Cardinal Joseph. *A Catholic Understanding of the Story of Creation and the Fall*. Grand Rapids, MI: Eerdmans, 1995.

————. *God and the World: A Conversation with Peter Seewald*. Translated by Henry Taylor. San Francisco: Ignatius Press, 2002.

————. *La Sal de la Tierra: Una conversación con Peter Seewald*. Madrid: Ediciones Palabra, 1997.

————. *God Is Near Us*. San Francisco: Ignatius Press, 2003.

Second Vatican Council. Pastoral Constitution *Gaudium et Spes*. December 7, 1965.

———. Constitution on the Sacred Liturgy *Sacrosanctum Concilium*. December 4, 1963.

———. Dogmatic Constitution on the Church *Lumen Gentium*, November 21, 1964.

———. Dogmatic Constitution on Divine Revelation *Dei Verbum*. November 18, 1965.

About the Author

Fr. John Portavella earned a doctorate in canon law from the University of Santo Tomas (Angelicum) in Rome. He was ordained in 1959 for the Opus Dei Prelature. He is currently doing pastoral work at the University of Asia and the Pacific, in Pasig City, Metro Manila.

Sophia Institute

Sophia Institute is a nonprofit institution that seeks to nurture the spiritual, moral, and cultural life of souls and to spread the Gospel of Christ in conformity with the authentic teachings of the Roman Catholic Church.

Sophia Institute Press fulfills this mission by offering translations, reprints, and new publications that afford readers a rich source of the enduring wisdom of mankind.

Sophia Institute also operates two popular online Catholic resources: CrisisMagazine.com and CatholicExchange.com.

Crisis Magazine provides insightful cultural analysis that arms readers with the arguments necessary for navigating the ideological and theological minefields of the day. *Catholic Exchange* provides world news from a Catholic perspective as well as daily devotionals and articles that will help you to grow in holiness and live a life consistent with the teachings of the Church.

In 2013, Sophia Institute launched Sophia Institute for Teachers to renew and rebuild Catholic culture through service to Catholic education. With the goal of nurturing the spiritual, moral, and cultural life of souls, and an abiding respect for the role and work of teachers, we strive to provide materials and programs that are at once enlightening to the mind and ennobling to the heart; faithful and complete, as well as useful and practical.

Sophia Institute gratefully recognizes the Solidarity Association for preserving and encouraging the growth of our apostolate over the course of many years. Without their generous and timely support, this book would not be in your hands.

www.SophiaInstitute.com
www.CatholicExchange.com
www.CrisisMagazine.com
www.SophiaInstituteforTeachers.org